THE U.S. PENSION CRISIS

THE U.S. PENSION CRISIS

What we need to do NOW to save America's pensions

Ronald J. Ryan, CFA

THE U.S. PENSION CRISIS

What we need to do NOW to save America's pensions

FIRST EDITION

www.ryanalm.com

ISBN: 978-0-615-28758-4

Library of Congress Control Number: 2012955305

Published by The Leading Press, an imprint of ExpressitMedia, LLC
Milton, DE 19968 | www.ExpressitMedia.com

Printed in the United States of America.

20 19 18 17 16 15 14 13 1 2 3 4 5 6 7 8 9 10

Dedication

This book is dedicated to all my employees,
who were so helpful and supportive of my career.
Special thanks to Martha C. Monteagudo,
who made my career and life so rewarding.

Ronald J. Ryan, CFA
CEO, Ryan ALM, Inc.

Preface

The crisis facing defined benefit pension plans in America today threatens the solvency and financial integrity of our corporations, our cities, our states, and even the U.S. government. The magnitude at which pension funds are underfunded suggests that this is the largest financial dilemma facing the U.S. since the Great Depression. In January 2005, Dr. Frank Fabozzi and I authored a special report in *Institutional Investor* magazine with the article: "Reforming Pension Reform." We identified the magnitude of the pension deficits at that time and the causes of such a dilemma. Since then, the pension dilemma has accelerated into a true national crisis.

In this book, I investigate in depth the true size and nature of the pension funding crisis, the causes of this disaster and, I pray, the potential solutions. My conclusion is that inappropriate accounting rules have misled pension plan sponsors into making inappropriate asset allocation decisions, inappropriate benefit decisions, inappropriate contribution decisions and inappropriate benchmarks. This caused a mismatch in risk/reward behavior between pension assets and pension liabilities, and ultimately the significant underperformance of pension assets vs. pension liabilities...it all links!

"The pen is mightier than the sword."

—Cardinal Richelieu

Table of Contents

CHAPTER ONE

THE HISTORY OF PENSIONS

According to Patrick W. Seburn's well-documented article "Evolution of Employer-Provided Defined Benefit Pensions" published in the December 1991 *Monthly Labor Review*,[1] the first private (i.e., corporate) pension plan began in 1875 with the American Express Company (then a shipping company). This newly created benefit was intended as an incentive to get workers to move to the West to work for long periods of time. Apparently, it worked. However, in order to qualify, retired employees had to have a minimum of 20 years' employment, had to be older than 60 years of age, and had to have a disability. Moreover, the general manager had to recommend retirement, and this recommendation was subject to approval by the company's executive committee of the board of directors. With these criteria, very few qualified. Those who did earned 50% of their last 10 year's average salaries with a cap of $500.[2] This plan was terminated in 1918, when the firm's express business was transferred to the American Railway Express Company. The American Railway Express Company continued to contribute to pensions on an informal

1 Patrick W. Seburn, "Evolution of employer-provided defined benefit pensions," *Monthly Labor Review* 114, no. 12 (December 1991): 16-23.

2 William C. Greenough and Francis P. King, *Pension Plans and Public Policy* (New York: Columbia University Press, 1976), 27.

basis while the American Express Company adopted a new plan in 1921.[3] By 1986, the American Express pension plan had evolved into an extensive program covering more than 23,000 employees—covering all retirees, not just the disabled. Employees had the option of retiring with a normal (i.e., unreduced) benefit at age 60 or retiring earlier with a reduction in the amount of the benefit, since it would be paid over a longer time.[4] And so it began, one of the greatest chapters in the history of employment benefits in America.

By 1880, the Baltimore and Ohio Railroad (B&O) established the first formal company-sponsored private pension plan to be financed jointly by both employer and employee contributions; it covered more than 77,000 workers. Perhaps the precursor to modern day pension plans benefit calculations, B&O pension benefits were computed by multiplying a portion of the employee's salary, usually for a period immediately preceding retirement, by a stated percentage. This result was then multiplied by the employee's years of service with the company. The B&O Railroad, the Central Railroad of New Jersey, and the Illinois Central Railroad were among the largest railroads of their day and had been in existence for at least 50 years prior to establishing their own pension plans. However, once initiated, interest in pension benefits spread quickly, and by 1916 more than half of all U.S. railroad employees were covered by railroad pension plans. Only a decade later, the proportion of railroad employees covered by these plans had risen to 80%.[5]

A major innovation in pensions occurred in 1921 when the Metropolitan Life Insurance Company offered the first group annuity contract.[6] This type of insurance contract made it possible to provide more workers with a post-retirement income less expensively than if each employee had to be individually insured. Both the employee and

3 Ibid., 28.

4 Internal Revenue Service, Form 5500 Annual Return/Report of Employee Benefit Plan (1986).

5 Pension Facts, 1987 (Washington, D.C.: American Council of Life Insurance, 1987).

6 Ibid., 33.

the employer benefited because the "risk" of an individual retiring and the cost of the plan were shared among many people, and the burden of administering a pension plan was lightened for the employer.

Another event helping to spur the growth in numbers of new private pension plans was the clarification of a plan's tax status contained in the Internal Revenue Act of 1921. Before 1921, employer contributions under a pension or other deferred compensation plan were not specifically exempt from Federal corporate income tax (instituted in 1915). However, it was common practice to allow firms to deduct such contributions as "ordinary and necessary business expenses," as long as the charges were deemed "reasonable." This informal practice was codified during the 1920s. In 1921, trusts created by employers as part of a stock bonus or profit-sharing plan for the exclusive benefit of some or all employees were made tax exempt. In addition, employer contributions to such trusts (and the income earned by them) would not be taxable to the beneficiaries until actually distributed. These provisions were extended to pension trusts in 1926. An estimated 3.7 million workers were covered in 1929.[7]

The greatest period of pension growth took place after 1940. Several factors promoted this increase. One was the clarification in 1942 of several sections of the Internal Revenue Code that dealt with pension trusts, in conjunction with an increase in normal and excess profits tax rates. The net effect was that an employer's contributions to a qualified pension plan were deductible for federal tax purposes in the determination of corporate income. Moreover, the federal government decided that employee earnings from a pension trust would not be federally taxed until after retirement, when the employee would presumably be in a lower tax bracket.

The second wartime development that influenced the growth of private pensions was the effort to curb inflation through general price controls. Because wages also were frozen, the only other type of

7 Murray W. Latimer, *Industrial Pension Systems in the United States and Canada* (New York: Industrial Relations Counselors, 1932), vol. 1, 230-31.

compensation with which employers could compete for scarce labor was employee benefits, which included pensions. Between 1940 and 1945, private pension plans added another 2.25 million active workers to their ranks.[8]

By the end of 1950, private pensions covered 10.3 million persons, representing more than one-fourth of all persons employed in commerce and industry in the United States. By year-end 1960, pension plans covered 23 million persons, about one-half of all private sector workers, and provided total retirement income in the amount of $1.7 billion annually.[9]

The changes in private pension plans that have occurred since 1875 have, in almost all cases, benefited the employee. Changes have resulted from employers' initiatives, collective bargaining, and pension legislation. The Employment Retirement Income Security Act (ERISA) enacted in 1974 has proved to be perhaps the single greatest influence on current pension plans. This act regulates almost every aspect of pension, profit-sharing, and thrift plans. Congress saw a need to establish legal standards that would guarantee benefits to workers covered by private pension plans. The main goal of the new ERISA Act is to protect employees' benefit rights as they relate to participation, funding, and vesting. ERISA affects all aspects of private pension plans, from creation to termination.[10]

The number of private pension plans in the United States increased twenty-fold in the decade after Congress passed the Social Security Act of 1935. However, most plans created in this period concentrated on high-compensation employees for whom public retirement benefits were thought to be inadequate. At the end of World War II, about 20% of private-sector employees participated in a pension plan.[11]

8 *Pension Facts*, 1987, 31.

9 *Pension Facts*, 1987, 32.

10 Evan L. Hodgens, "Key changes in major pension plans," *Monthly Labor Review* (July 1975), 25-26.

11 Internal Revenue Service, *Form 5500 Annual Return/Report of Employee Benefit Plan* (1986).

During the 1980s, pension plan assets grew rapidly, while employee benefits increased only slightly. By 1980, almost 180,000 defined benefit pension plans, funded by $400 billion in assets, covered 38 million active workers. By 1987, more than 232,000 defined benefit pension plans covered nearly 40 million participants, and the assets of these plans reached nearly $900 billion.

After 135 years, the pension industry has become one of the largest assets in America. Accordingly, pension liabilities have also become one of the greatest debts in America. *Pensions & Investments* September 30, 2010, survey reports that of the 1,000 largest defined benefit plans in the U.S., 223 were public plans and 615 were private plans, for a total in assets of $3.924 trillion:[12]

EXHIBIT 1

	# of Plans	Size of Assets
Public Plans	223	$2.540 trillion
Private Plans	615	$1.384 trillion
Total		**$3.924 trillion**

For most cities, states, and major corporations with defined benefit plans, the pension asset is their largest asset and the pension liability is their largest debt. Unfortunately, pension contribution costs together with pension benefit payments have also become one of their major budget costs and certainly the fastest growing. Note that such costs are not included in the Consumer Price Index (CPI), even though employees quite often pay their share of contribution costs (an increasing trend).

According to the February 2011 study by Towers Watson, **U.S. pension assets total $14.265 trillion—a figure equal to 100.23% of the U.S. Gross Domestic Product (GDP)** (see Exhibit 2).[13] As was

12 "The P&I 1,000," *Pensions & Investments* (Feb. 7, 2011).

13 Towers Watson, *Global Pension Asset Study 2011* (February 2011).

mentioned earlier but well worth repeating, for most pension plan sponsors, the pension asset is their largest asset, and the pension liability is their largest liability. Accounting rules rank pension liability as senior debt.

EXHIBIT 2

ESTIMATED 2012 GROSS DOMESTIC PRODUCT ($ MILLION)			
1. United States	$14,231,300	**6. France**	$2,242,740
2. Japan	4,690,050	**7. Italy**	1,717,710
3. China	4,503,520	**8. India**	1,410,920
4. Germany	3,040,520	**9. Canada**	1,257,810
5. United Kingdom	2,334,160	**10. Spain**	1,167,560

Source: USDA[14]

Pensions should be viewed as part of the total compensation of an employee. Indeed, such a compensation package can be a strong incentive for someone to work for an employer and remain in the position for a considerable period of time. It is quite possible, if not probable, that future pension compensation could exceed the wages earned over any employee's business career. Defined benefit plans promise to pay defined benefits that are formula-based and forecastable. As a result, many employees budget for their future life based on their retirement package. Any disruption in their retirement payment schedule could seriously compromise the standard of living of those employees who planned their retirement on these pension promises.

"It is amazing what you can accomplish if you do not care who gets the credit."

—Harry Truman

14 United States Department of Agriculture, *Real Historical and Projected Gross Domestic Product (GDP) and Growth Rates of GDP for Baseline Countries (in billions of 2005 dollars) 1969-2030* (December 2013).

CHAPTER **TWO**

THE PENSION OBJECTIVE

The stated objective of any pension plan is to fund liability payments in such a way that contribution costs remain stable and low over the future pension horizon. Contribution costs are the extra funds that pension plan sponsors are required to contribute to reach an annual fully funded status. Such contribution costs are in addition to the pension benefit payments. The New York City Employees' Retirement System (NYCERS) actuarial report says it well in every annual report:

> *The financial objective of the New York City Employees' Retirement System (the "Plan") is to fund members' retirement benefits during their active service and to establish employer normal contribution rates that, expressed as a percentage of active member annualized covered payroll, would remain approximately level over the future working lifetimes of those active members and together with member contributions and investment income, would ultimately be sufficient to accumulate assets to pay benefits when due.*[15]

15 2009 Annual Report, New York City Employees' Retirement System, 126.

Clearly, the pension objective is one of funding liabilities in such a way that contribution costs remain low and stable over the future. The reason this current pension dilemma is a crisis is that it became a significant budget expense (i.e., cost crisis) for so many cities and states, as well as a growing pension expense and liability item for corporations, affecting earnings and balance sheets. Due to spiking pension contribution costs, most cities and states were not prepared for such budget escalations, which resulted in deep budget deficits and deteriorating credit ratings. Corporations were also hit with higher pension expenses and higher contribution costs that affected earnings, credit ratings, and even solvency. As funded ratios eroded, growing unfunded liabilities (deficits) were created, which reduced the creditworthiness of their balance sheets.

The employer (i.e., pension plan sponsor) is responsible for the benefit payments and the administration of the pension. **The pension plan sponsor's objective is to fund these pension liabilities at a low and stable cost with prudent risk to the plan.** Pension cost is viewed and managed as the cost of contributions plus benefits paid. Unfortunately, such costs tend to be a large and ever-growing cash expense that affects budgets and creditworthiness. For private plans, cost also includes the line item pension expense that directly affects earnings (as explained in Chapter 8: Phantom Earnings). As such, how the pension cost affects earnings (private plans) and budgets (public plans) plays a major role in how pension plans are managed.

Indeed, the House of Representatives held a hearing on Feb. 14, 2011, titled "The Role of Public Employee Pensions in Contributing to State Insolvency and the Possibility of a State Bankruptcy," which raised the question: Will America face a rash of municipal bankruptcies? The answer should be a resounding NO!

Although the budget deficits are monumental, there are actions that can be, should have been, and have been taken. Cutting the budgets is the first. New Jersey has taken the lead here with a 5% cut across the board in 2010. Kudos to New Jersey Gov. Chris Christie and his legislature. The second is raising taxes, a politically sensitive but effective step. A good example is Illinois whose leaders raised 2011 state personal income taxes by 67% (from 3% to 5%) and also raised business income taxes by 46% (from 4.8% to 7%) to help erase a $13 billion state budget deficit. The third is to sell or lease the valuable assets most cities and states possess (i.e., buildings, roads, tunnels, and the like). Although not very liquid, these assets are a good source of capital. Fourth and most important, is to correct the pension deficits. Again, the cause of most of these huge budget deficits is the rising contribution costs stemming from a mismatch of pension asset growth versus liability growth. Notably, the cost of annual pension contributions is close to (and possibly higher than) 100% of most city and state budget deficits. Therefore, if municipalities could correct their pension deficits, they would repair their budget deficits.

Required sponsor contribution costs are mainly the result of pension asset growth being insufficient to fund the annual pension benefit payments. To calculate annual contributions, pension liabilities are first discounted at a specific rate to create a present value. For public plans, Government Accounting Standards Board (GASB) and Actuarial Standards of Practice (ASOP) use the Return on Assets (ROA) assumption as the discount rate. The present value of assets and liabilities is then projected to grow at the ROA. Any annual shortfall (deficit) in projected asset value vs. projected liability value is funded by an Annual Required Contribution (ARC), which is an added pension cost factor. Perhaps the clearest example of such escalating contribution costs is provided by the New York City Employees' Retirement System (NYCERS), one of five New

York City pension funds. Exhibit 3 shows the history of their contribution payments.[16]

EXHIBIT 3

HISTORY OF NYCERS CONTRIBUTION COSTS

Fiscal Year Ended	Annual Required Contribution	Employer Rate of Contribution
6/30/00	$ 68,619,745	0.915%
6/30/01	100,024,692	1.271
6/30/02	105,660,069	1.241
6/30/03	107,992,496	1.213
6/30/04	310,589,074	3.526
6/30/05	822,763,025	8.985
6/30/06	1,024,358,175	11.142
6/30/07	1,471,029,609	15.556
6/30/08	1,874,242,487	19.001
6/30/09	2,150,438,042	20.570
6/30/10	2,197,717,073	20.020
6/30/11	2,387,215,772	20.820
6/30/12	3,017,004,318	25.540

Amazingly, NYCERS contribution costs increased more than 43 times in 12 fiscal years, equal to 37.07% annual growth. **The employer rate of contribution escalated from 0.915% to 25.54% of payroll!**

16 Michael A. Goldson, et al., *Comprehensive Annual Financial Report for the Fiscal Years Ended June 30, 2012* and June 30, 2011, 180. https://www.nycers.org/%28S%28n5jda02ztcksmbvy1lf4y155%29%29/Pdf/cafr/2012/CAFR2012.pdf.

How could any budget keep up with such rising costs, especially when they are not foreseen or even understood? Why did pension contribution costs explode? How do we solve this problem and prevent this trend from ever surfacing again? These are compelling questions and problems that I have labored for many years to explore in order to find the appropriate answers and solutions. This is my story of the U.S. Pension Crisis.

The sole purpose of growing and protecting pension assets is to secure the payment of defined pension benefits (liabilities) at specified benefit dates and at low cost with prudent risk. **Indeed, funding pension liabilities at low and stable costs is the true objective of pension plans. It is a cost objective, not a return objective!** However, attention to the pension liability objective is not evident in most pension plans. Noticeably, liabilities are missing in action with regard to every major asset function; they are typically not found in asset allocation, asset management, and performance measurement.

Asset allocation models are focused on achieving an *absolute* rate of return (usually the return on asset assumption or ROA) rather than a *relative* growth rate versus the growth rate of liabilities. Moreover, most pension asset managers are given a generic market index as their benchmark, which usually has no correlation or similarity to the behavior pattern of liabilities. If the equity asset manager outperforms the S&P 500, does that mean these assets outperformed the liability growth rate? Of course not! If any asset manager outperforms his *generic* market index benchmark (bogey), does that mean those assets have outgrown liabilities and are funding liabilities correctly? Of course not! With the exception of zero coupon bonds matched to liabilities, all other assets are usually not correlated to liabilities, with most non-bond asset classes producing a negative correlation. It has become commonplace that pension asset managers are given objectives of outperforming the growth rate of generic market indices, or the ROA (Return on Asset assumption = static absolute return target) instead of outgrowing liability growth. Liability growth is a volatile return behavior similar to long Treasuries and is best measured by a custom liability index. There is no evidence that any generic market index or ROA target behaves like pension liabilities. This sets up the obvious conclusion that has plagued the pension industry: **that the wrong objective (ROA or generic benchmark index) produces the wrong risk/reward outcome!**

In God We Trust!
(Not in our financial institutions.)

CHAPTER **THREE**

THE PENSION CRISIS FACTS

Depending on the accounting method you report under, or what study you pick, public and private pensions have a combined deficit of from $800 million to over $4 trillion! If TARP I was a national emergency at $800 billion, what do we call this current pension deficit situation? Here are the calculations from recent studies.

Pew Report on States[17]

In February 2010, The Pew Center released "The Trillion Dollar Gap," a report based on fiscal 2008 data for state pension plans. The report calculates a public pension deficit (for states only) of $452 billion, or a funded ratio of 84% on assets of $2.3 trillion. This number is derived from the information that states reported, which was based on ***actuarial*** valuations rather than ***market*** valuations. Exhibit 4 shows some of the key findings:

17 The Pew Charitable Trusts, *The Trillion Dollar Gap* (Feb. 18, 2010). http://www.pewtrusts.org/our_work_report_detail.aspx?id=57353.

EXHIBIT 4

Pew Center Study	
Fully Funded Ratio:	26 states (2000) 4 states (2008) = FL, NY, WA, WI
Funded Ratio < 80%:	21 states
Funded Ratio < 67%:	8 states (CT, IL, KA, KY, MA, OK, RI, WV)
Worst Funded Ratio:	Illinois = 54% ($54 billion deficit)

Source: The Pew Charitable Trusts, *The Trillion Dollar Gap* (Feb. 18, 2010).

From such declining funded ratios come increasing contribution costs. Any shortfalls (deficits) are made up for through higher contributions. Known as the Annual Required Contribution (ARC), this is the amount of money actuaries calculate that the employer needs to contribute to the plan during the current year in order to fully fund benefits.

In fiscal 2000 (ending June 30) when pensions were well-funded, states had to pay $27 billion to adequately fund promised benefits. By fiscal 2008, states pension contributions had grown to $64 billion, a 135% increase from 2000. Unfortunately, in the last five years, 21 states failed to make the full ARC payment. According to Pew, 21 states skipped $6.6 billion in contributions for fiscal year 2008. Exhibit 5 shows the Pew listing of state pension funding levels and the resulting contributions using data as of fiscal 2008.

EXHIBIT 5

PEW 2010 REPORT OF STATE FUNDING LEVELS ($ 000S)
(2008 FISCAL YEAR DATA EXCEPT FOR OHIO = 2007)

State	Pension Liability	Unfunded Liability	ARC	Actual Contribution
Alabama	40,206,232	9,228,918	1,069,214	1,069,214
Alaska	14,558,255	3,522,661	282,656	300,534
Arizona	39,831,327	7,871,120	1,028337	1,035,557
California	35,956,264	59,492,498	12,376,481	10,469,213
Colorado	55.625,011	16,813,048	1,141,081	779,644
Connecticut	41,311,400	15,858,500	1,248,860	3,243,647
Delaware	7,334,478	129,359	149,614	144,358
Florida	129,196,897	1,798,789	3,005,387	3,130,378
Georgia	75,897,678	6,384,903	1,275,881	1,275,881
Hawaii	16,549,069	5,168,108	488,770	510,727
Idaho	11,526.600	772,200	256,400	285,400
Illinois	119,084,440	54,383,939	3,729,181	2,156,267
Indiana	35,640,073	9,825,830	1,232,347	1,275,191
Iowa	24,552,217	2,694,794	453,980	389,564
Kansas	20,106,787	8,279,168	607,662	395,588
Kentucky	34,094,002	12,328,429	859,305	569,913
Louisiana	38,350,804	11,658,734	1,160,051	1,337,933
Maine	13,674,901	2,782,173	305,361	305,361
Maryland	50,561,824	10,926,099	1,208,497	1,077,796
Massachusetts	58,817,153	21,759,452	1,226,526	1,368,788
Michigan	70,354,300	11,514,600	1,249,909	1,392,709
Minnesota	57,841,634	10,771,507	1,036,509	767,295
Mississippi	29,311,471	7,971,277	662,900	643,356
Missouri	52,827,423	9,025,293	1,219,871	1,072,027
Montana	9,632,853	1,549,503	201,871	211,914
Nebraska	8,894,328	754,748	169,068	169,068
Nevada	30,563,852	7,281,752	1,262,758	1,174,837
N Hampshire	7,869,189	2,522,175	251,764	189,134
New Jersey	25,807,485	34,434,055	3,691,740	2,107,243
New Mexico	26,122,238	4,519,887	667,691	591,279
New York	141,255,000	10,428,000	2,648,450	2,648,450
N. Carolina	73,624,027	504,760	675,704	675,056
North Dakota	4,193,600	546,500	80,928	59,900

(continued on next page)

State	Pension Liability	Unfunded Liability	ARC	Actual Contribution
Ohio	148,061,498	19,502,063	2,632,521	2,369,045
Oklahoma	33,527,899	13,172,407	1,245,646	986,163
Oregon	54,260,000	10,739,000	707,400	707,400
Pennsylvania	105,282,637	13,724,480	2,436,486	986,670
Rhode Island	11,188,813	4,353,892	219,864	219,864
So. Carolina	40,318,435	12,052,684	902,340	902,365
South Dakota	7,078,007	182,870	95,766	95,766
Tennessee	32,715,771	1,602,802	838,259	825.259
Texas	148,594,953	13,781,228	1,871,409	1,854,968
Utah	22,674,673	3,611,399	641,690	641,690
Vermont	3,792,854	461,551	83,579	78,743
Virginia	65,164,000	10,723,000	1,486,768	1,375,894
Washington	54,322,900	179,100	1,545,600	967,900
West Virginia	13,642,584	4,968,709	481,703	510,258
Wisconsin	80,758,800	11,306,231	152,973	125,438

Source: The Pew Charitable Trusts, *The Trillion Dollar Gap* (Feb. 18, 2010).

I need to reiterate that the Pew report uses data as reported by each state. Such data is based on Government Accounting Standards Board (GASB) accounting and Actuarial Standards of Practice (ASOP) actuarial valuations, and not market valuations. Asset valuations are generally calculated on a five-year average, a process referred to as smoothing. Liability valuations are calculated using a discount rate equal to the ROA (at 8.00%). If we were to use current *market valuations* for 2008, assets would be 10% to 20% less, and liabilities would be 40% to 60% higher.

Center for State and Local Government Excellence

The Center for State and Local Government Excellence released their Issue Brief on 126 state and local pension plans in June 2010. They calculated an aggregate pension liability of $3.4 trillion as of 2009 data based on GASB 25 accounting, which uses the ROA as the discount rate (at 8%). Assets were $2.7 trillion, suggesting an unfunded liability of $0.7 trillion. However, using a more conservative discount rate of 5.0% would increase liabilities to $4.9 trillion and the **unfunded liability would be near $2.2 trillion.**[18] If the risk-free Treasury STRIPS yield curve was used as the discount rates as of 12/31/09 (at 4.3% for 10-year and at 4.87% for 15-year STRIP) the liability valuation would be 2% to 7% higher ($ 5.24 trillion) and the unfunded liability would be near $2.54 trillion.

Study by Profs. Robert Novy-Marx and Joshua Rauh

Supporting my estimate of a $3 trillion Public Plan deficit is the study by Profs. Robert Novy-Marx, University of Rochester, and Joshua Rauh, Kellogg School of Management. Their study suggests that if zero coupon Treasury yields are used as the risk-free discount rates, the unfunded liability would be roughly $3 trillion for state-sponsored pension plans and $383 billion for cities, for a **combined unfunded liability of $3.383 trillion!**[19] They have since revised their estimates to over $4 trillion.

IRS Form 5500 and Credit Suisse

Based on IRS form 5500, corporate pension plans were underfunded by about $465 billion at the end of 2004. Based on the Credit Suisse pension update released on Oct. 10, 2011, its pension forecast model

18 Alicia H. Munnell et al., *Issue Brief: Valuing Liabilities in State and Local Plans, Center for State & Local Government Excellence* (June 2010).

19 Robert Novy-Marx and Joshua Rauh, "The Crisis in Local Government Pensions in the United States" (Brookings-Nomura-Wharton Conference *Growing Old: Paying for Retirement and Institutional Money Management after the Financial Crisis*, October 2010).

estimated the funded status of the 354 companies in the S&P 500 with defined benefit plans to be 72% funded (or $477 billion underfunded) using the FASB accounting methods. Credit Suisse also estimates that companies will face pension contributions of $91 billion in 2012 vs. $52 billion in 2011. They find that **the median increase in estimated contributions for 2012 is up 76%.**[20]

Conclusion

Thus, for both corporate and public pension funds, there are strong arguments to be made that **pension liabilities are greatly *understated*, funded ratios are *overstated*, and therefore pension deficits are even larger and more serious than reported.** The level of contributions is the litmus test as to whether pension plans are worse off than five to 10 years ago. For most pensions (especially public), contributions have spiked upward at an alarming rate.

"Things are going to get a lot worse before they get worse."

—Lily Tomlin

20 David Zion, Amit Varshney, and Nichole Burnap, *From Bad to Worse* (New York: Credit Suisse Securities (USA) LLC, 10 October 2011).

CHAPTER **FOUR**

SOCIAL CONSEQUENCES

The current pension dilemma is so large and complex that it affects almost every American's way of life, from the business arena to social circles, **causing us to face the greatest financial challenge in U.S. history. How we solve the Pension Crisis will shape our economy for generations to come.** The ripple effect of growing pension deficits and spiking contribution costs has affected most layers of the American way of life.

Taxes

Government leaders are usually reluctant to raise taxes, as the practice is not welcomed by the voting public. However, when faced with critical and immediate budget problems, politicians have little choice but to raise some type of tax revenue. As mentioned in Chapter 2, elected officials in Illinois raised 2011 state personal income taxes by 67% (from 3% to 5%) and also raised business income taxes by 46% (from 4.8% to 7%) to help erase a $13 billion state budget deficit.

Budgets

City and state leaders should cut expenses when faced with critical budget deficits, especially when the expenses are huge and growing.

New Jersey has taken the lead in cutting budgets with a 5% cut across the board in 2010. This means potentially reduced services for New Jersey residents, possibly affecting quality of life standards and certainly employment within the State.

Pension Benefit Guaranty Corp (PBGC)[21]

The PBGC is the government organization that takes over a pension plan when a corporation files for bankruptcy. The PBGC charges an annual insurance premium of $35 per employee for such protection. However, this premium is increased by $9 per $1,000 of unfunded vested benefits (0.90%) when a corporation has an unfunded pension deficit. This is an additional cost to corporations of $900,000 per $100 million of unfunded vested benefits, which hurts earnings. The PBGC also has a benefit cap of $55,841 per employee annually. Therefore, any employee who earned and expected a pension benefit greater than $55,841 would have a reduced benefit package for the rest of his life. In 2002, the PBGC was supporting 3,122 plans with 344,310 participants at a cost of $1.54 billion annually. As of fiscal 2012, the PBGC has taken over 4,292 pension plans affecting 775,300 participants with benefits paid totaling $5.34 billion annually. This represents a 148.3% increase in the number of participants, costing the PBGC an additional 247.4% in benefit costs over the last 10 years. Since the PBGC is a federal agency, any budget deficits become added costs to the American taxpayer. As of fiscal 2012 (ending Sept. 20, 2012) the PBGC reported a $26 billion deficit—the largest in its 38-year history.

Stocks

For most major corporations, the pension asset is the largest asset of the firm, and the pension liability is the largest debt of the firm.

21 Pension Benefit Guaranty Cooperation: A U.S. Government Agency. http://pbgc.gov.

This plays a major role in the financial statements. Pension expense (benefits and contributions) plus actuarial losses resulting from poor pension asset performance (returns below ROA estimate) are a direct hit to the earnings of a corporation. As a result, pensions play a role in the stock valuation. Since 1999, companies dragged down by the costs of their pensions represent a growing trend. As the PBGC reports, over 1,000 company pensions were taken over by the PBGC from 2002 to 2011 due to bankruptcies. In too many cases, the cause of such bankruptcy was the burden of pension expense.

Creditworthiness

Pensions affect the credit ratings of cities, states, and corporations. Due to the current 12-year trend (since 1999) of deteriorating funded ratios, such entities are faced with ever-increasing debt (unfunded pension liabilities). For most cities and states, this increasing pension debt has damaged their credit worthiness making their cost of borrowing more expensive. As reported by *Business Insider* in April 2009, **for the first time ever, Moody's placed all municipal issuers on their negative watch list.**[22]

Trend to Frozen Pension Plans and Defined Contribution

Given the spiking contribution costs and the financial statement ignominy attributable to pension expenses since 1999, corporations have been on a fast track to discard the defined benefit (DB) compensation by freezing the defined benefit plan, and replacing it with a defined contribution (DC) plan (also known as a 401k) for new employees. According to a Towers Watson study of the Fortune 100 retirement plans, there was a dramatic 48% shift away from DB to DC plans from 1985 to 2010.[23]

---

22 Joe Weisenthal, "Moody's Downgrades the Whole Country," *Business Insider* (Apr. 8, 2009).

23 Insider, Towers Watson, June 2010. http://www.towerswatson.com/en-US/Insights/Newsletters/Americas/insider/2012/retirement-plan-type-of-fortune-100-companies-in-2012.

FORTUNE 100 RETIREMENT PLANS				
	1985	**1998**	**2005**	**2010**
DB Plans	90	90	63	42
DC Plans	10	10	37	58

Another study by Towers Watson also demonstrated a strong trend toward freezing defined benefit plans among the Fortune 1000 companies.[24]

	# of DB Sponsors	**# of Sponsors with Frozen Plans**	**% Frozen**
2009	607	190	31.3
2008	624	169	27.1
2007	638	138	21.6
2006	627	113	18.0
2005	627	71	11.3
2004	633	45	7.1

By freezing their defined benefit plans, companies are either closing off benefits to new employees (a soft freeze) or halting all future benefits accruals for existing employees (a hard freeze). Defined benefit plans base pension benefits on a formula typically based on average salary and tenure. The longer the tenure and the higher the salary, the greater the benefits. Unfortunately, it's no longer viable for most companies to provide such expensive compensation. Companies are not required by law to offer or maintain a defined benefit pension plan. The shift to defined contribution plans transfers the responsibility and asset allocation risk to the employee, who makes personal decisions regarding contribution amounts and specific investment

24 Watson Wyatt, *Pension Freezes Continue Among Fortune 1000 Companies in 2009*, Towers Watson August (2009). http://www.watsonwyatt.com/us/pubs/insider/showarticle.asp?ArticleID=21857.

strategies. Companies are required to provide at least three defined contribution investment options: principal preservation, principal appreciation, and income.

Social Security and Medicare

Although this book focuses on public and private pension plans, most Americans are only too familiar with the monumental deficits of Social Security and Medicare, which are primarily funded through the FICA tax on payroll. It would be wise to pay attention to how this tax grows in the foreseeable future. Starting in 2013, the Social Security tax portion will increase from 4.2% to 6.2% (a 47.6% increase) and the Medicare tax portion will increase from 2.9% to 3.8% (a 31.0% increase) for individuals with salaries exceeding $200,000 or married couples exceeding $250,000.[25] In addition, there is an alarming demographic trend that is difficult to correct: The baby boomer generation is now becoming a dependent generation, increasing the number of retirees eligible for Social Security benefits. Meanwhile, the number of workers who pay the FICA tax has been in a slow but steady decline for decades.

RATIO OF SOCIAL SECURITY COVERED WORKERS TO BENEFICIARIES

Year	Covered Workers (000s)	Beneficiaries (000s)	Ratio
1940	35,390	222	159.4
1950	46,390	1,106	41.9
1960	72,530	14,262	5.1
1970	93,090	25,186	3.7
1980	113,656	35,118	3.2
1990	133,672	39,470	3.4
2000	155,295	45,166	3.4
2010	156,725	53,398	2.9

25 Trust Fund Data, www.ssa.gov/history/ratios.html.

Should this trend continue, the payroll tax burden on current FICA tax payers will almost certainly increase to pay for the benefits of the retired generation. Considering the current massive deficits of both the Social Security and Medicare programs, it's anyone's guess as to where the FICA tax will go. Unfortunately, it seems to be nearly certain that the FICA tax rate will need to rise significantly over the next 20 years.

"We all have to play the ball as it lies."

—Bobby Jones

CHAPTER **FIVE**

"WOODY" THE PENSION PENCIL

The Weapon of Mass Destruction in Pension America

There are numerous rules, regulations, and regulatory bodies involved in the pension game, including GASB, FASB, PPA, the Employee Retirement Income Security Act of 1974 (ERISA), and the Internal Revenue Service (IRS), just to name a few. Although confusing and tiresome, these rules dictate how the pension game has been and will be played. Indeed, it is my view that such rules (especially the accounting rules) are the major cause of the pension crisis we face today. One of the great difficulties in managing pensions is understanding the accounting and actuarial rule jabberwocky that seems to plague this industry. Such rules are undergoing revision and rethinking today that will seemingly produce more practical applications over time. However, as in sports, the better the pension rules are understood, the better the pension game can be played. Therefore, we need to review these cumbersome rules to comprehend how the pension game has been and should be played. Solving a financial problem is difficult if you do not know what the problem truly is.

When I testified before the ERISA Committee in 2003[26] (to read my complete testimony, see p. 173), I brought in a five-foot pencil that I introduced as "Woody" the pension pencil. I consider Woody the weapon of mass destruction in financial America. Indeed, if you thought Enron and WorldCom had magic accounting pencils that led to their debacles, wait till you see what the pension accounting pencil Woody has done to budgets, balance sheets, and income statements. In the following chapters, I will demonstrate how Woody is used in GASB and FASB accounting rules to reduce contribution costs, and enhance funded ratios, earnings, and balance sheets.

> ***"Investors should be skeptical of history-based models. Beware of geeks bearing formulas."***
>
> —Warren Buffett

26 Ronald J. Ryan, Testimony before ERISA Advisory Council on Employee Welfare and Pension Benefit Plans (July 24, 2003).

CHAPTER **SIX**

"WOODY" THE PUBLIC PENSION PENCIL: GOVERNMENT ACCOUNTING STANDARDS BOARD (GASB)

The Government Accounting Standards Board (GASB) governs accounting for state and local pension plans. GASB 25/27 is the set of accounting rules for public pensions. Public pensions can point to GASB as a major villain of their budget problems. These inappropriate accounting rules misled pensions through inappropriate valuations of both pension assets and liabilities. This caused the funded ratios (or present value of assets/liabilities) to be greatly exaggerated, which led to inappropriate asset allocation, benefit and contribution decisions—they all link!

Instead of marking to market, GASB uses our friend "Woody" to allow public pension plans to smooth assets over a moving five-year average. Smoothing of assets was mandated by GASB as a way to remove volatility from budgets and contribution costs. In the end, the opposite occurred as contribution costs spiked upward beginning in 2000. Imagine if your bank reported your financial statements in this manner. Would you be comfortable writing a check for an amount that's based on a five-year smoothed balance, instead of on your current market balance?

Using the static asset allocation model shown in Exhibit 7, I have estimated pension asset growth based on smoothing over a five-year average (Exhibit 8).

EXHIBIT 7

Asset Allocation Model (*Static*):	
Cash (Ryan Cash Index)	5%
Bonds (Lehman/Barclays Aggregate)	30%
Stocks (S&P 500)	60%
Int'l Stocks (EAFE)	5%

EXHIBIT 8

Total Returns from Smoothing of Assets over 5 years			
2000	= 14.50%	**2007**	= 10.45%
2001	= 10.03	**2008**	= 7.95
2002	= 3.15	**2009**	= 3.69
2003	= 2.88	**2010**	= 5.16
2004	= 1.93	**2011**	= 3.39
2005	= 3.52	**2012**	= 8.83
2006	= 6.84		

It is easy to see that smoothing produced a consistent positive return for assets that was in sharp contrast to the reality: **pension assets experienced the worst total returns in their history over a decade.** When used to calculate the funded ratio and contributions, smoothing exaggerated the funded ratio and reduced contribution costs inappropriately. Such erroneous calculations were part of the misleading accounting valuations that misled pension plans into inappropriate asset allocation, benefits and contribution decisions... **it all links!**

Exhibit 9 shows my estimate of the market value growth rates of pension assets and liabilities for the last 13 years ending 12/31/12 using the asset allocation of Exhibit 7 versus the Ryan Liability Benchmark Index (Ryan 1-30 years STRIPS indexes equally weighted).[27] The volatility of assets and liabilities is easy to see when using market values (economic values). Also note the significant and consistent underperformance of asset growth versus liability growth, which accumulates to -194.30% return difference (16.25% annual average) over those 13 years (2000-2012). As a result, the funded ratio drops 55.14% to 44.86% from its 12/31/99 starting level of 100%. In order to avoid a deficit under this scenario, pensions would have had to have a funded ratio of 225.77% as of 12/31/99 (see Exhibit 9).

EXHIBIT 9

ASSETS VS. LIABILITIES GROWTH RATES (THE RYAN LETTER)

Year	Assets	Liabilities	Annual Difference	Cumulative Difference	Funded Ratio %
2000	-2.50	25.96	-28.46	-28.46	77.41
2001	-5.40	3.08	-8.48	-37.60	71.04
2002	-11.41	19.47	-30.88	-73.40	52.68
2003	20.04	1.96	18.08	-60.08	62.01
2004	8.92	9.38	-0.43	-66.13	61.76
2005	4.43	8.87	-4.44	-76.75	59.25
2006	12.25	0.81	11.44	-64.60	65.97
2007	6.82	11.76	-4.94	-78.38	63.22
2008	-24.47	33.93	-58.40	-183.08	35.56
2009	19.43	-19.52	38.95	-107.99	52.77
2010	11.89	10.13	1.76	-116.80	53.62
2011	3.27	33.77	-30.50	-197.41	41.39
2012	11.79	4.46	7.33	-191.63	44.86

27 Ryan ALM, Inc., "The Ryan ALM Pension Letter", December 2012.

Exhibit 10 compares the GASB accounting value (smoothing assets) as shown in Exhibit 8 versus the economic value of assets (market value) as shown in Exhibit 9. This clearly shows the considerable return disparities (-64.61% cumulative overvaluation) just on the asset valuation side, which would lead to erroneous funded ratio calculations.

EXHIBIT 10

GROWTH RATE: ASSETS SMOOTHED VS. ASSETS MARKET VALUE

Year	Assets Smoothed	Assets MV	Annual Difference	Cumulative Difference
2000	14.50	-2.50	17.00	17.00
2001	10.03	-5.40	15.43	33.74
2002	3.15	-11.41	14.56	48.24
2003	2.88	20.04	-17.16	35.61
2004	1.93	8.92	-6.99	29.44
2005	3.52	4.43	-0.91	29.50
2006	6.84	12.25	-5.41	25.49
2007	10.45	6.82	3.63	32.69
2008	7.95	-24.47	32.42	78.67
2009	3.69	19.43	-15.74	65.67
2010	5.16	11.89	-6.73	60.93
2011	3.39	3.27	0.12	63.16
2012	8.83	11.79	-2.96	64.61

Notice that in the last 13 years, the smoothing methodology produced consistent positive total returns. This was in sharp contrast to the reality of the market's roller coaster behavior of deep negative growth years (2000-2002 and 2008) and high positive growth years (2003 and 2009). Smoothing overvalued assets in six years (2000-2002, 2007, 2008, and 2011) and undervalued assets in six years (2003-

2006, 2009-2010), thereby cumulatively overvaluing assets by 64.61% over 13 years (110.49% smoothed versus 55.88% economic). Annual disparities ranged from being 32.42% overvalued (2008) to being -17.16% undervalued (2003). Since contributions are an annual calculation, smoothing did not reduce the volatility of contributions as intended. More importantly, smoothing helped to create an erroneous funded ratio which led to misinformed asset allocation, benefits and contribution decisions...**it all links!**

Based on the market valuations shown in Exhibit 9, pension assets would have grown by 55.88% and pension liabilities would have grown cumulatively by 247.51% over the period 12/31/99 through 12/31/12. Therefore, by my estimate, pension liabilities should have outgrown pension assets by about 191.63% cumulatively over the last 13 years. This would have caused funded ratios to deteriorate by -55.14%, requiring a funded ratio of 225.77% in 1999 in order to be fully funded by 2012. Such difference in asset growth versus liability growth is depicted in the tables in Exhibits 13 and 14 (the type of which appear routinely in *The Ryan ALM Pension Letter* distributed quarterly). Exhibit 11 on the next page shows the 12-month moving average growth difference, while Exhibit 12 shows the cumulative growth difference. Moreover, given a deficit, assets have to grow at a faster rate to catch up to liabilities. A funded ratio of 50% suggests that assets have to grow twice as fast as liabilities to catch up, and a 75% ratio requires 33% more asset growth.

The biggest problem with GASB accounting is that it allows for pension liabilities to be valued at a discount rate equal to the Return on Asset (ROA) assumption. Based on the study by the Center for State and Local Government Excellence,[28] the average ROA used by public pensions is 8%. Such an ROA tends to be a static and robust projection. As a result, GASB has liability growth at a steady 8.00% annual growth. This annual growth rate is in sharp contrast to the

28 *Valuing Liabilities in State and Local Plans*, Center of State and Local Government Excellence (June 20, 2010).

history of liability market value growth rates (shown in Exhibit 13, p. 34), which are quite volatile with high positive and high negative annual market value growth rates (Ryan Liability Benchmark Index = Ryan Treasury STRIPS 1-30 year indexes equally weighted).

EXHIBIT 11

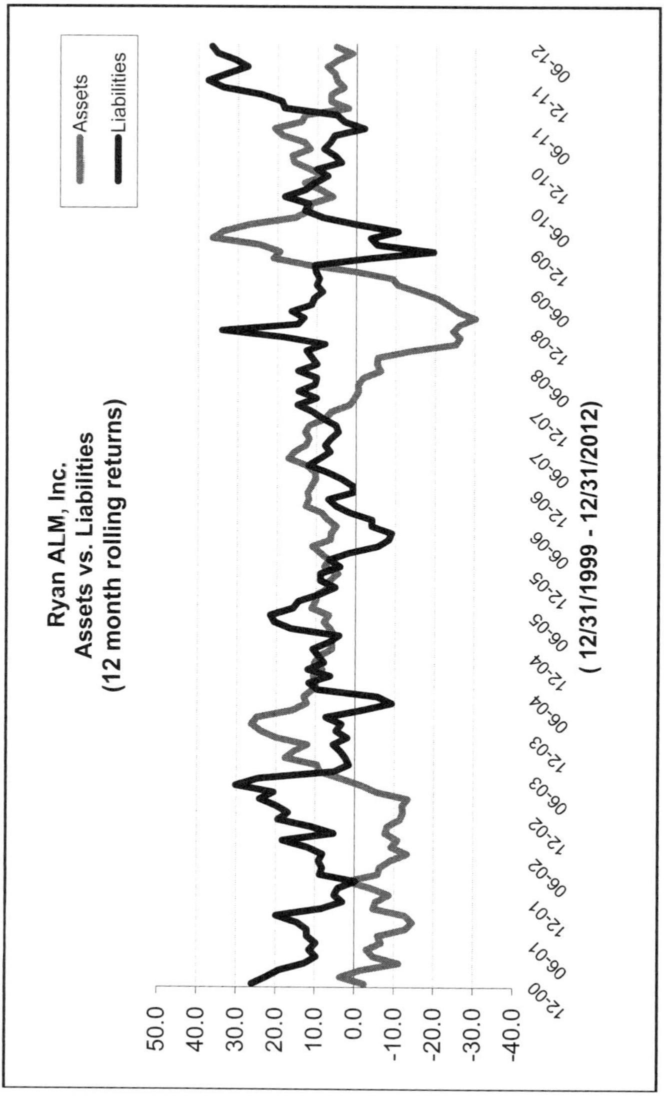

EXHIBIT 12

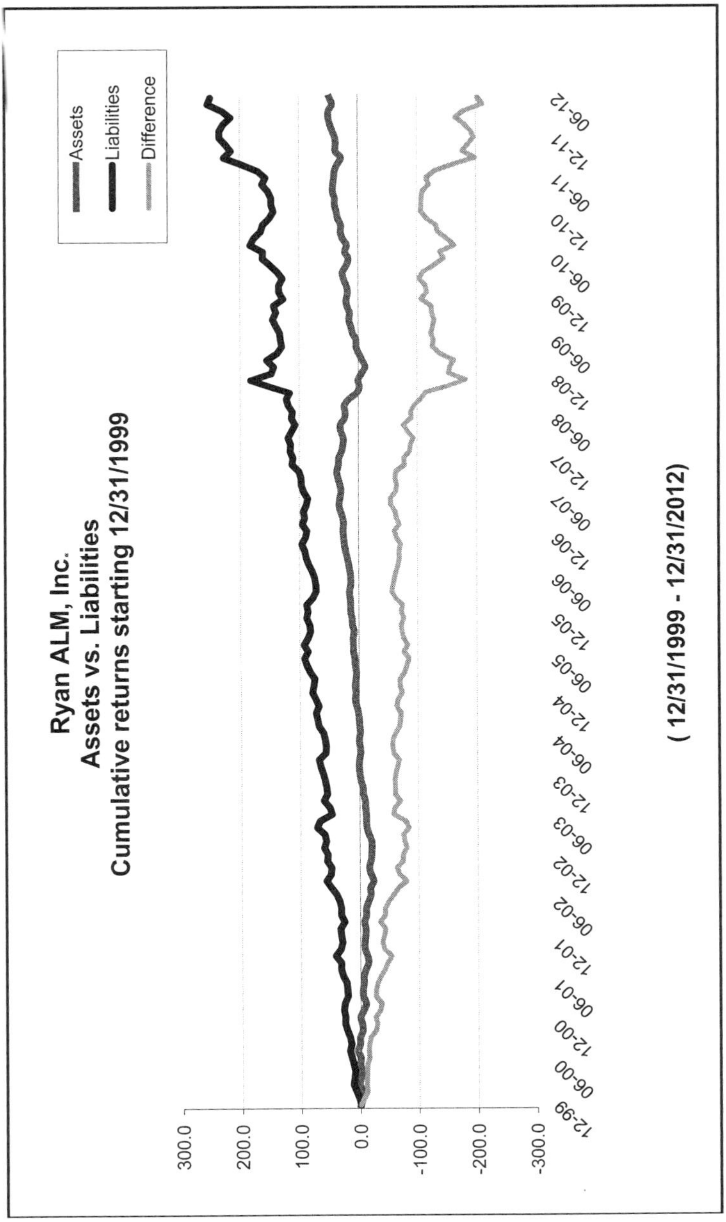
Ryan ALM, Inc.
Assets vs. Liabilities
Cumulative returns starting 12/31/1999
Assets
Liabilities
Difference
300.0
200.0
100.0
0.0
-100.0
-200.0
-300.0
12-99
06-00
12-00
06-01
12-01
06-02
12-02
06-03
12-03
06-04
12-04
06-05
12-05
06-06
12-06
06-07
12-07
06-08
12-08
06-09
12-09
06-10
12-10
06-11
12-11
06-12
(12/31/1999 - 12/31/2012)

EXHIBIT 13

RYAN LIABILITY BENCHMARK INDEX GROWTH RATES (%)

1989									
25.40									
1990	**1991**	**1992**	**1993**	**1994**	**1995**	**1996**	**1997**	**1998**	**1999**
3.23	19.26	7.87	22.46	-12.60	41.60	-3.70	19.63	16.23	-12.70
2000	**2001**	**2002**	**2003**	**2004**	**2005**	**2006**	**2007**	**2008**	**2009**
25.96	3.08	19.47	1.96	9.35	8.87	0.81	11.76	33.93	-19.52
2010	**2011**	**2012**							
10.13	33.77	4.46							

Given that interest rates are quite volatile, the GASB accounting rules ignore reality and true economic valuations. Even less realistic is the present value calculation of liabilities used to calculate the funded ratio. Since most pension benefit payment schedules have an average life (duration) of between 10 and 15 years, comparing the 10-year and 15-year Treasury STRIPS yields to the GASB approach of an 8% ROA discount rate would be an appropriate proxy for pension liabilities' present value differences. As Exhibit 14 on the following page indicates, using the ROA approach as a single discount rate significantly ***undervalues*** **the present value (PV) of liabilities by 24% to over 70%, which then exaggerates the funded ratio (assets/liabilities).**

The combination of smoothing assets, which *overvalued* assets in the decade of the 2000s, plus using the ROA as the discount rate, which *undervalued* liabilities, significantly **exaggerated the reported funded ratio by 19% to 41%.** Such an exaggerated funded ratio hypothetically reduces any reported deficit, which supposedly reduces contribution costs. This is why the ROA is favored over much lower discount rates (i.e., Treasury market rates)—it *supposedly* lowers contribution costs.

EXHIBIT 14

PRESENT VALUE DIFFERENCE (MARKET VS. GASB)				
	Market Yield to Maturity		Market vs. GASB PV Difference vs. ROA	
	10 year	15 year	10 year	15 year
Year End	STRIPS	STRIPS	STRIPS	STRIPS
2000	5.30%	5.67%	27.0%	35.0%
2001	5.59%	6.06%	24.1%	29.1%
2002	4.34%	5.09%	36.6%	43.7%
2003	4.63%	5.32%	33.7%	40.2%
2004	4.49%	4.97%	35.1%	45.5%
2005	4.51%	4.68%	34.9%	49.8%
2006	4.80%	5.01%	32.0%	44.9%
2007	4.39%	4.69%	36.1%	49.7%
2008	2.98%	3.33%	50.2%	70.1%
2009	4.20%	4.87%	38.0%	47.0%
2010	3.66%	4.41%	43.4%	53.9%
2011	2.06%	2.73%	50.94%	52.7%
2012	1.92%	2.63%	60.8%	53.7%

PV Difference = (GASB yield – STRIPS yield) x Duration

Using NYCERS as our model again in Exhibit 15, it becomes clear that a funded ratio distortion was created by GASB accounting rules and actuarial valuations that comply with GASB 25/27 and Actuarial Standards of Practice 27 (ASOP 27). Fortunately, NYCERS communicates the market-related value of plan assets (MVA) versus the market value of the ABO liabilities (MVABO), so any board trustee can see the distortion quite clearly between market value (MV) and actuarial value (AV). However, NYCERS provides eight different funded ratio calculations, which might confuse most trustees unless they are sophisticated or well-taught. Exhibit 15 shows how NYCERS reported their 12-year funded ratio history from fiscal year 2000 through fiscal year 2011 (ending June 30) based on these different calculations.

EXHIBIT 15

NYCERS FUNDED RATIOS

Fiscal Year	AAV/AAL	AAV/ABO	MVA/MVABO
1999	100%	169%	138%
2000	100	146	120
2001	100	143	97
2002	100	135	80
2003	100	124	64
2004	100	114	75
2005	100	109	64
2006	100	101	75
2007	100	97	79
2008	100	97	65
2009	100	96	48
2010	100	93	48
2011	100	75	44

Legend: AAV = Actuarial Asset Valuation
AAL = Actuarial Accrued Liability
ABO = Accrued Benefit Obligation discounted at GASB rates (8%)
MVA = Market Value of Assets
MVABO = Market Value of ABO

Source 2011 NYCERS Comprehensive Annual Financial Report

Exhibit 16 on the following page contains an excerpt from the 2011 NYCERS Comprehensive Annual Financial Report (CAFR), which provides eight distinct funded ratio calculations. A public pension board of trustees needs to be astute as to what is being reported here. The differences in valuations are alarming, as the 6/30/10 fiscal year shows a funded ratio based on market value (MVA/MVABO) at 48% vs. the 93% reported using actuarial values (AAV/ABO).

EXHIBIT 16

NEW YORK CITY EMPLOYEES' RETIREMENT SYSTEM

ADDITIONAL DISCUSSION OF PLAN FUNDING AND
OTHER MEASURES OF FUNDED STATUS
(Cont'd)

Table of Funded Ratios

The following table presents alternative Funded Ratios comparing Assets to Obligations, including: (1) AAV divided by AAL, (2) AAV divided by EAAL, (3) MVA divided by EAAL, (4) AAV divided by PBO, (5) MVA divided by PBO, (6) AAV divided by ABO, (7) MVA divided by ABO and (8) MVA divided by MVABO.

Funded Ratios								
Valuation Date	AAV/AAL	AAV/EAAL	MVA/EAAL	AAV/PBO	MVA/PBO	AAV/ABO	MVA/ABO	MVA/ MVABO
6/30/99	100%	136%	136%	148%	148%	169%	169%	138%
6/30/00	100	122	123	133	134	146	148	120
6/30/01	100	117	102	129	111	143	123	97
6/30/02	100	112	84	123	93	135	102	80
6/30/03	100	104	78	114	85	124	93	64
6/30/04	100	95	81	105	89	114	97	75
6/30/04 (Lag)	100	94	79	104	87	116	97	75
6/30/05 (Lag)	100	88	79	97	87	109	97	64
6/30/06 (Lag)	100	82	80	90	88	101	98	75
6/30/07 (Lag)	100	79	86	87	95	97	106	79
6/30/08 (Lag)	100	80	78	87	85	97	95	65
6/30/09 (Lag)	100	79	60	86	66	96	73	48
6/30/10 (Lag)#	100	77	64	84	70	93	78	48

Preliminary.

Legend: AAV = Actuarial Asset Valuation
AAL = Actuarial Accrued Liability
ABO = Accrued Benefit Obligation discounted at GASB rates (8%)
MVA = Market Value of Assets
MVABO = Market Value of ABO

As presented in the NYCERS actuarial report, the funded ratio was reported much higher (and even consistently fully funded) using actuarial values (AAV/PBO and AAV/ABO) rather than market value accounting (MVA/ MVABO) which shows a continuous erosion of the funded ratios (from a high of 138% in fiscal 1999, to a low of 48% in fiscal 2009 and 2010) and deep deficits starting in fiscal 2003. This led to an exaggeration of the funded ratio. Such an erroneous and overstated funded ratio is common among public pension plan sponsors and misled many to increase benefits and reduce contributions when they couldn't afford either one (note years 2002 through 2010). Such an exaggerated funded ratio was described by Elizabeth Kellar, president of the Center for State and Local Excellence, in the organization's June 2010 Issue Brief:

> *"What caught my eye was the CalPERS pension history they cite. In 1997, CalPERS reported that assets equaled 111 percent of liabilities using the traditional actuarial model. That upbeat report led the California legislature to enhance the benefits of both current and future employees. The legislature reduced the retirement age, increased benefit accrual rates, and shortened the salary base for benefits to the final year's salary. If CalPERS liabilities had been valued at the riskless rate in 1997, the plan would have been 76 percent funded. The authors suggest that a riskless rate of valuing liabilities would minimize the temptation for elected officials to become overly generous in good financial times and would better protect funding levels when there is a downturn."*[29]

Indeed, GASB accounting rules were established to avoid volatility in contribution costs by smoothing assets and keeping liability

29 Elizabeth K. Kellar, "President's Letter," *Issue Brief: Valuing Liabilities in State and Local Plans* (Center for State and Local Government Excellence, June 2010), 2. http://slge.org/publications/valuing-liabilities-in-state-and-local-plans

growth a constant (i.e., static ROA discount rate). However, in the end, these accounting rules created erroneous funded ratios, volatile and spiking contribution costs, added benefit costs, and inappropriate asset allocation by misleading pensions as to the proper economic valuation of their funded ratios and the needed target asset return... it all links!

The worst consequence of the GASB accounting rules may be their effects on asset allocation, benefit, and contribution decisions... it all links to the ROA! Because GASB assigned the liability growth rate as the ROA, and actuaries use the ROA to calculate contributions, the ROA became the target growth rate for assets. To understand the logic of this, one need only examine the way that actuaries calculate projected contribution costs. The Annual Required Contribution (ARC) is the balancing item between the annual projected future values of assets versus liabilities to reach full funding. Actuaries grow the assets at the ROA. Liabilities are first discounted at the ROA (i.e., present value) and then grow at the ROA (i.e., future value). Note that liabilities have the same growth rate (ROA) as the assets! This means that the projected contribution calculation assumes that only through contributions (future assets) can assets match or fully fund liabilities, since assets and liabilities have the same projected growth rate. Total unfunded liabilities (liabilities minus assets) is then amortized over the 20 to 30 funding policy years. **In fact, the only true value of the ROA is to calculate contributions—it is *not* a pension asset hurdle rate or benchmark growth rate!**

Pension plan sponsors are told that when assets don't grow at the ROA level, they create an actuarial and GASB accounting deficit that is funded through extra contributions. This is not correct thinking, or correct math. If there is a deficit, then even if the assets grow at the ROA, contribution costs *will* go up! If a deficit exists, assets must *outgrow* liabilities in order to reduce contribution costs and reach full funding. For example, given assets of $60 and liabilities of $100, there is a 40% shortfall. Obviously, if they both grow at an ROA of 8%, since 8% of $60 is less than 8% of $100, a greater dollar deficit results, while the funded ratio remains at 60%. Such a growing dollar deficit requires a higher contribution to reach full funding.

In Exhibit 17, with a funded ratio of 60%, in just six short years of assets and liabilities both growing at 8%, the deficit increases over 58%. Accordingly, assets have to *outgrow* liabilities to reduce contribution costs. In fact, in this example, assets have to outgrow liabilities by 5.33% per year (equal to a 13.33% ROA, 67% higher than an 8% ROA) for contribution costs to remain level, although at a high rate.

EXHIBIT 17

EXAMPLE: FUNDED RATIO = 60% (40% DEFICIT)

	Growth Rate = 8% ROA				Deficit	
Year	**Assets**	**$ Growth**	**Liabilities**	**$ Growth**	**$**	**% Increase**
1	$60.00	$4.80	$100.00	8.00	43.20	8.00%
2	64.80	5.18	108.00	8.64	46.66	16.65
3	69.98	5.60	116.64	9.33	50.39	25.98
4	75.58	6.05	125.97	10.07	54.42	36.05
5	81.63	6.53	136.05	10.88	58.77	46.93
6	88.16	7.05	146.93	11.72	63.44	58.60

Requires ROA = 13.33% to not increase contribution costs
Assets > Liability growth by 5.33% = Level contributions

With a surplus position, assets don't need to work as hard as the ROA. If assets just match true economic liability growth, they will secure the surplus. This is the rationale behind immunization strategies, which are highly recommended when funded ratios are fully funded on an economic basis, or market value. Exhibit 18 shows a 140% funded ratio with assets of $100 and liabilities of $71.43. Naturally, if both grow at 8% (ROA), 8% of $100 will be greater than 8% of $71.43, thereby creating a growing surplus in funds with no contribution costs (in other words, a pension holiday) although the funded ratio will remain constant at 140%. Assets could grow at -2.28% less than liabilities without creating a contribution cost over the six years shown. However, the true target return should be to match or hedge liability growth in market values, not actuarial values. This is best accomplished with a custom liability index (CLI) and liability beta portfolio, both of which are explained in more detail in Chapter 15 Asset Liability Management.

EXHIBIT 18

EXAMPLE: FUNDED RATIO = 140% (40% SURPLUS)

	Growth Rate = 8% ROA				Contributions	
Year	**Assets**	**$ Growth**	**Liabilities**	**$ Growth**	**$ Cost**	**% Increase**
1	$100.00	$8.00	$71.43	$5.71	$NA	
2	108.00	8.64	77.14	6.18	NA	
3	116.64	9.33	83.32	6.66	NA	
4	125.97	10.07	89.98	7.20	NA	
5	136.05	10.88	97.18	7.77	NA	
6	146.93	11.72	104.95	8.40	NA	

Requires an ROA = 5.72% for NO contribution costs
Assets < Liability growth by -2.28% = NO contribution

In truth, assets and liabilities never grow at the ROA, therefore the ROA is a poor forecaster of growth that leads to a lot of bad decisions... it all links! The real problems start with asset allocation. The ROA needs to be validated by an asset allocation model. Usually, the pension consultant is required to construct an asset allocation that has the highest probability of achieving the ROA. Asset allocation models use an optimization technique based on the average returns from long historical index databases (at 20 years) for every asset class but one: bonds, which go into the asset allocation models at their *current yields*. In the decade of the 1990s, most pension funds enjoyed growing pension surpluses wherein they reduced, if not eliminated, contribution costs. Benefit increases were also a beneficiary of these good times. One would think that prudent pension investors would have altered their asset allocation to include more bonds matched to liabilities (i.e., used an immunization strategy) to secure their victory and lock in reduced contributions for the future. But **asset allocation models are based on achieving the ROA and never consider the funded ratio—a fatal flaw**. When bond interest rates fell below the ROA of 8% in the late 1980s, bonds became a drag on achieving the ROA, so the asset allocation models reduced their allocation to bonds in what became a consistent trend. By 1999, most asset allocation models had the lowest allocation to bonds in modern history and the highest allocation to equities—**the $3.4 trillion mistake!**[30] When the equity correction occurred in 2000 through 2002, public pensions were hard hit due to their asset allocation skewness to equities. Most pension equity assets underperformed liability growth by over 70% in just those three years. Based on the S&P 500 and the Ryan Liability Benchmark,[31] the S&P 500 underperformed liabilities by 75.88% in three short years (2000-2002) as shown in Exhibit 19.

EXHIBIT 19

EQUITY GROWTH VS. LIABILITY GROWTH

	2000	2001	2002	Cumulative
S&P 500 Index	-9.09	11.86	-22.08	-20.76%
Ryan Liability Index	25.96	3.08	19.47	55.12
				-75.88%

30 Robert Novy-Marx and Joshua Rauh, "The Crisis in Local Government Pensions in the United States." Brookings-Nomura-Wharton Conference Growing Old: Paying for Retirement and Institutional Money Management after the Financial Crisis (October 2010).

31 Ronald J. Ryan, *Portable Alpha . . . Redefined* (Ryan ALM, Inc., December 31, 2007). http://www.ryanalm.com/portals/5/research/portable-alpha-redefined.pdf.

The Boards of Trustees for public pension funds were given reports that communicated their funded ratio based on GASB accounting and actuarial valuations and not on economic reality (i.e., market values). Such GASB accounting *overstated* assets by over 16% due to *smoothing*, and *undervalued* liabilities by 24% to 70% by using the ROA as the discount rate instead of market rates, since 1999. Thanks, Woody! This caused a severe exaggeration of the funded ratio, such that many pension plan sponsors increased benefits and reduced contributions at a time when they could not afford either. The Pension Protection Act (PPA) is a great example of effective rules that require private pensions to have a high funded ratio based on market values *before* benefits can be increased. This is a proper test.

Even the Actuarial Standards Board (ASB) in their release of *Actuarial Standard Practice* (No. 27, Section 3.6) acknowledges that the ROA may not be appropriate for unfunded pensions:

> Section 3.6 Selecting an Investment Return Assumption and a Discount Rate
>
> *Generally, the appropriate discount rate is the same as the investment return assumption. But for some purposes, such as SFAS No. 87 or unfunded plan valuations, the discount rate may be selected independently of the plan's investment return assumption.*[32]

Most pension plan sponsors have been brainwashed into thinking that the ROA is both their focus and the target asset growth rate. Had pensions matched asset to liabilities using high quality zero coupon bonds in the late 1990s, they would have secured fully funded positions for their futures thereby reducing or even eliminating contribution costs. **The focus of pensions should be their**

32 Actuarial Standards Board, *Actuarial Standard of Practice No. 27: Selection of Economic Assumptions for Measuring Pension Obligations*, (adopted September 2007; revised ed. May 1, 2011), 5. http://www.actuarialstandardsboard.org/pdf/asops/asop027_145.pdf.

funded ratio, and not the ROA. A surplus funded ratio should have a radically more conservative asset allocation (i.e., immunization strategy) than a deficit position in order to secure the surplus and reduce contribution costs long term. But in the 1990s and 2000s the opposite took place because of a secular trend towards lower interest rates. When investment grade bond interest rates fell below the ROA, bonds became a drag on achieving the ROA target in asset allocation models. As a result, these models skewed asset allocation increasingly away from bonds and into more risky securities. By 1999, most pension asset allocations had the lowest allocation to bonds and the highest exposure to domestic equities in modern history. When the equity correction hit in 2000 through 2002, asset values were hard hit due to this heavy allocation to domestic equities—hence, the $3.4 trillion asset allocation mistake!

GASB Invitation To Comment (ITC)[33]

GASB sent out an ITC April 6, 2009, on pension accounting and financial reporting. Below is the response I sent to GASB in answer to question 5b:

> QUESTION: What should be the basis for determining the discount rate used for discounting projected pension benefits to their present value for accounting purposes? Why?
>
> ANSWER: **Pension liabilities should always be valued at the risk-free Treasury STRIPS yield curve** rates for numerous reasons and benefits:
>
> - **Only a zero coupon bond has a certain future value and can be used as a discount rate(s).** This is well-documented by defeasance strategies, pre-fundings of municipal bonds, lotteries, FAS 87, FAS 106, and FAS 158. **The only**

33 Ronald J. Ryan, Answers to GASB ITC: *Invitation to Comment* (June 12, 2009).

zero coupon *yield curve* that you can buy to defease liabilities is the Treasury STRIPS yield curve. All others are hypothetical and cannot be purchased (i.e., financial creations). Agency zeroes exist (but not as a yield curve from one issuer), plus they have some credit risk (i.e., FNMA, FHLMC, FICO, REFCO, TVA, etc.).

- *Each* liability payment should be priced to calculate its present value. Accordingly, you need a yield curve of discount rates that can match the cash flow or benefit payment schedule. Only the Treasury STRIPS yield curve offers rates monthly or quarterly out 30 years.

- The ROA (long-term investment yield) is a *forecast* of asset returns—a very bad forecast. The ROA never predicts negative returns and merges all asset classes into one return assumption. Since it is not a yield curve, it has nothing to do with the behavior of liabilities. By definition, using the ROA as the discount rate creates a flat and static yield curve that is updated infrequently (annually). This is in sharp contrast to the true behavior of interest rates and liabilities. In reality, yield curves are dynamic shapes that are forever changing (inverse, positive sloping, etc.), which would affect the present values of liabilities and funded ratios.

- The ROA usually is a higher discount rate than risk-free Treasury STRIPS. This not only undervalues the present value of liabilities, but overvalues the funded ratio and causes an unwarranted reduction in contributions, which damages the future solvency of the plan.

- The ROA has become the hurdle rate or target rate for public pension assets. This causes asset allocation models to be heavily skewed to non-bonds while being quite static. Moreover, it tends to persuade asset allocation into more risky investments to meet the ROA target. As a result, in the late 1990s when most pension plans had surpluses, plan sponsors and pension consultants did not change their asset allocation to bonds matched to liabilities because doing so would not validate or match the ROA. Had they switched their asset allocation to bonds matched to liabilities, they would have secured their surplus position. This static asset allocation led to the disastrous decade of the 2000s. Amazingly, most state lotteries mandate that all assets be in Treasury zero coupon bonds matched to their liabilities. Thanks to this asset/liability matching requirement, we never hear of a problem with state lotteries.

- **The funded ratio (market value of assets/market value of liabilities) should be the focus of asset allocation.** A surplus should have a different asset allocation than a deficit. Until pensions "mark to market" both the assets and liabilities in a frequent and accurate manner, the true economic funded ratio will not be known. The true objective of the asset side should be to enhance the economic funded ratio and reduce contribution costs. Isn't it amazing how many public plans show a fully funded or near fully funded plan, while contributions have increased dramatically in this decade? (See New York city employees.) How could you be fully funded, and have your contribution costs go up significantly every year? Pensions are misled about their true economic conditions and unfortunately behave accordingly. If you are told you are fully funded, you may decide to increase benefits or decrease contributions at a time when you cannot afford to do so. This is a common malady facing most public pension funds.

- The **Society of Actuaries** 2004 research explained that until pension plans create a set of economic books (market value), asset management cannot achieve its financial objective of funding liabilities.[34]

- I testified before the **ERISA Committee** twice. I urged that the pension accounting rules should state clearly that discount rates must be real rates such that you must prove that you can buy the discount rates used so that the reporting pension plan has the knowledge and ability to defease liabilities at those rates (and cost) if they so desire. Rates that are not purchasable are financial creations or lies that distort the economic reality of the plan's liabilities and funded ratio. An overvalued funded ratio due to a much higher discount rate than the true economic reality leads to erroneous asset allocation, benefit and contribution decisions. This is the pension crisis of today.

- The **borrowing rate** of an employer should never be used as a discount rate for many obvious reasons. First, it creates a bias towards lower credits. The higher the yield, the lower the present value, suggesting that the same liability payment schedule for one borrower is worth less than another. Second, there are usually no zero coupon bonds for most issuers. Third, there would never be enough supply of zeroes for the pension to buy if it wanted to match liabilities. Fourth, it would not be operating at "arm's length"

---

34 Charles L. Gilbert, *Principles Underlying Asset Liability Management* (Society of Actuaries Task Force on Asset Liability, Oct. 12, 2004).

if a pension bought heavily the bonds of the plan sponsor. Usually, investment policies prohibit or limit such transactions to 5% of assets.

"Where is the knowledge we have lost in information?"

—T.S. Eliot

CHAPTER **SEVEN**

"WOODY" THE PRIVATE PENSION PENCIL: FINANCIAL ACCOUNTING STANDARDS BOARD (FASB)

The Financial Accounting Standards Board (FASB) governs the accounting statements for corporations in America. As a result, such accounting rules play a key role in the report of earnings (income statement) and solvency (balance sheet). Since pensions tend to be the largest asset and the largest liability of most mature companies, they can significantly influence such financial statements. Companies and their stock prices are *earnings* led, not *liability* led. This is not a problem unless it leads to manipulation of the financials in a way that is not ethical or is immoral (e.g., WorldCom and Enron). Unfortunately, and certainly not intentionally, the history of FASB rules and their interpretation have tended to distort earnings and liabilities as they apply to pension accounting.

The initial FASB pension rules were released in December 1985 and became fully effective in 1987 with FAS Statement No. 87. Some highlights were that Statement No. 87 reaffirms the usefulness of information based on *accrual accounting*. Accrual accounting goes beyond cash transactions to provide information about assets, liabilities, and earnings. FASB believes that an employer with an *unfunded* pension obligation has a liability, and an employer with an *overfund-*

ed pension obligation has an asset. The most relevant and reliable information available about that liability or asset is that it is based on the fair value of plan assets and a measure of the present value of the obligation using current, explicit assumptions.[35] FASB governs the financial statements of private corporations with FAS No. 87 and governs pension accounting with FAS No. 158. Since the defined benefit plan tends to be one of the largest liabilities of any major corporation, the size and how well-funded these plans are have a major impact upon the solvency of corporations. It is amazing how large pension liabilities are relative to the market capitalization of corporations, as Exhibit 20 proves:

EXHIBIT 20[36]

ESTIMATED PROJECTED BENEFIT OBLIGATION (PBO) / MARKET CAP (DATA AS OF SEPTEMBER 15, 2010, IN $ MILLIONS)

	2010E PBO	Market Cap	PBO / Mkt. Cap
Eastman Kodak	8,816	1,021	864%
Goodyear	8,641	2,626	329%
AK Steel	3,590	1,507	238%
Ford Motor	72,596	39,984	182%
New York Times	2,119	1,199	177%
U.S. Steel	10,341	6,572	157%
Northrop Grumman	26,689	17,062	156%
Lockheed Martin	37,836	24,824	152%
Boeing	58,355	45,898	127%
Textron	5,780	5,185	111%
Supervalue	2,600	2,338	111%
Alcoa	12,594	11,672	108%
Int'l Paper	10,606	10,008	106%
Gannett	3,317	3,197	104%
Donnelley	3,562	3,449	103%

Source: Crecit Suisse

35 FASB, "Summary of Statement," *Statement of Financial Accounting Standards No. 87* (Norwalk, CT: Financial Accounting Standards Board, 1986). http://www.fasb.org/summary/stsum87.shtml.

36 David Zion, Amit Varshney, "Pension Headwinds", Credit Suisse Group AG (Sept. 21, 2010). www.credit-suisse.com.

FASB Rules

FASB does a better job of explaining how pension liabilities work and how they should be priced than GASB. FAS No. 87, paragraph 44, deals with the valuation of pension liabilities:

> *"Assumed discount rates shall reflect the rates at which the pension benefits could be effectively settled . . . In making those estimates, employers may look to rates of return on high-quality fixed income investments currently available and expected to be available during the period to maturity of the pension benefits."* [37]

It seems pretty clear that FASB is stating that the discount rates to be used to price and value liabilities should be a yield curve of rates (individual discount rates) that *settle* each liability benefit payment. This is the language of "defeasement" (the exact matching of liabilities with assets such that the liabilities are pre-funded or defeased). Moreover, FASB states that such discount rates must be from high-quality bonds that are available to the benefit payment dates. This translates into non-callable bonds that are high-quality for life. It would seem then, that only U.S. Treasury securities qualify under these FASB rules. What other bonds could be high-quality for life? It then follows that since the only high-quality, non-callable bonds for life (maturity) are Treasuries, pension liabilities should be priced off the Treasury yield curve. Moreover, FASB notes that such discount rates should *settle* the liabilities. The translation here is that the discount rates to be used are such that you can purchase these discount rates to defease or fund liabilities (i.e., settle the liabilities). Pension plans should match the maturity dates of these high-quality bonds to the pension benefit payment dates as a yield curve or term structure of discount rates. **Since only zero coupon bonds have a**

37 FASB, *Statement of Financial Accounting Standards No. 87* (Norwalk, CT: Financial Accounting Standards Board, 1986), par. 44

certain future value, they are the only securities that could ever match the future value of liabilities with certainty and, as a result, are favored as defeasance and immunization strategies. In today's market, we are limited to mostly government zero coupon bonds since there are very few corporate zero coupon bonds and certainly no well-defined and liquid high quality corporate zero coupon yield curve.

Since government bonds tend to be the lowest yielding bonds, this would cause the present value of liabilities to be higher than using corporate bonds. The natural reaction from corporations was that government bond pricing of their pension liabilities would hurt their financial statements, funded ratios and contribution costs. They looked for a better methodology, and found what they thought was an answer: the Moody's Aa Corporate Bond Index.

Moody's Aa Corporate Bond Index

The Moody's Aa Corporate Bond Index was invented way back in 1929. It was a rather strange index, but after the release of FAS No. 87, it became a popular source for pricing liabilities of defined benefit plans for corporations. The major reason for its use seems to be that it was the highest yielding published rate that seemed acceptable under FAS No. 87 guidelines. The Moody's rules for calculating this rate were:

Composition	Portfolio of approximately 16 bonds
Maturities	20 years + (average = 30 years)
Rating	Only Aa bonds by Moody's (all levels)
Industries	Industrials and Utilities (no Finance)
Pricing	Only bonds near par (pricing from $95 to 105)

Such a bond index was loaded with structural problems, but no one seemed to care as long as it gave the desired answer or yield. The list of structural difficulties was lengthy:

1. **Yield Curve.** By definition, the Moody's Aa Corporate Rate is a "spot" on the corporate bond yield curve, namely 20+ years. As a result, it is not a yield curve and incapable of pricing most liabilities. Any single discount rate is certainly not an accurate pricing methodology. Moreover, it violates FAS No. 87, paragraph 199, which clearly states that a yield curve of individual discount rates is to be used.

2. **No Zero Coupon Bonds.** There were no zero coupon bonds in the corporate bond portfolio comprising the Moody's Aa rate calculation. This suggests that such a rate is **not** in conformity with FASB rules and the guidance directed by the SEC (to follow FAS No. 106 guidelines, paragraph 186).

3. **No Finance.** An oddity of this rate calculation is the absence of finance issues that comprised about 49% of the corporate bond market and about 20% of the long corporate area during the late 1980s through the 1990s.

4. **Current Coupons.** Moody's focuses on bonds supposedly priced close to par to best represent the current coupon market. This was difficult to find as only 16 issues qualify and only 44 bonds were Aa with maturities longer than 20 years by 2000. Moreover, this is certainly not representative of the current market with most long bonds priced well above $105.

5. **Defeasance.** The true test of any liability pricing methodology is whether the rates used can be purchased to defease the liabilities. Obviously, this is "mission impossible" here since such Moody's Aa rates do not exist below a 20-year maturity, nor do they exist past 15-year duration (only government zero

coupon bonds exist past a 15-year duration out to a 30-year duration).

6. **Transparency.** Moody's did not publish the portfolio of bonds. This was available by subscription only for an annual fee. To be an industry standard, such rates should be easily attainable with complete statistics and information supporting such calculations.

7. **Yields.** The quoted yield is an **average yield** for the month and not the month-end close. Since rates tend to be volatile and the size of pension liabilities significant, for every 10 basis points of rate error or difference, approximately 1% to 1.5% liability valuation difference in present value dollars would result. As a result, Moody's Aa rate is not an accurate pricing methodology.

8. **Call Features.** Moody's selection criteria are based on maturity even if the bonds are priced to call date. Supposedly, using bonds close to par (prices from $95 to $105) negates this situation.

9. **Weights.** Moody's equal weights the issues within two industry sectors (industrials and utilities). By 2000, there were 10 industrial issues and six utility issues. The weighted average yields for these two industry sectors are then equally weighted to determine the total average yield. Since industrials tend to trade much richer than utilities, this calculation has a bias towards creating a higher average yield.

To be fair, Moody's never intended for this rate to be a liability-pricing model. It was initially constructed way back in 1929 and its survival for several decades was a testimony to the industry acceptance of Moody's data. It is the accounting practitioners who used this rate, perhaps inappropriately. Moreover, the Moody's rate is not an index, in the sense that it does not calculate total returns.

FAS No. 87 continued...

Given the structural weaknesses of the Moody's Aa rate, private pension plans needed to look elsewhere for proper discount rates. FASB was quite detailed in explaining which discount rates qualify. For example, paragraph 199 of FAS No. 87 reads:

> *"Interest rates vary depending on the duration of investments; for example, Treasury bills, 7-year bonds and 30-year bonds have different interest rates... The disclosures required by this Statement regarding components of the pension obligation will be more representationally faithful if individual discount rates applicable to various benefit deferral periods are selected."* [38]

FASB is very clear here that *individual discount rates* should be used. In other words, each liability should be priced individually off of a *yield* curve with the same maturity as the liability benefit payment date (i.e., liability matching or defeasance discount rate methodology). Once again, FASB is emphasizing the use of a yield curve as the discount rate methodology. A *single* discount rate or an *average* discount rate is not in conformity to FASB rules here.

The SEC and FAS No. 106

In 1993, the SEC became involved when it questioned a registrant (Caterpillar) about the selection of discount rates they used under FAS No. 87. The SEC wrote a letter to the corporation and FASB stat-

38 FASB, *Statement of Financial Accounting Standards No. 87* (Norwalk, CT: Financial Accounting Standards Board, 1986), par. 199.

ing that "the SEC staff believes that the guidance provided in paragraph 186 of FAS No. 106 for selecting discount rates to measure the post-retirement benefit obligation also is appropriate guidance for measuring pension obligations." The SEC further specified, "rates that cannot be justified or are just too high will be passed on to the SEC's enforcement division for further action. The enforcement division could require restatement of the company's financial statements, as well as seek to impose **civil or criminal penalties**."[39]

Wow! The SEC is declaring that using inappropriate and too high a discount rate(s) is a **potential crime**! Indeed, on financial statements it is considered "fraud" (e.g., Enron and WorldCom). Since pension liabilities tend to be very large relative to the total debt and net worth of companies, any accounting treatment that misvalues and reduces the true economic value of such pension obligations could significantly distort the reported funded ratio and creditworthiness of such firms. To provide guidance on pension discount rates so as to protect companies from wrongdoing, the SEC is instructing companies to follow FAS No. 106, paragraph 186. Since FAS No. 106 was created for medical Other Post Employment Benefits (OPEB liabilities), this seemed unusual. Apparently, according to the SEC, the present value of both pension and medical OPEB liabilities should be discounted in the same manner. FAS No. 106, paragraph 186 reads:

> *The objective of selecting assumed discount rates is to measure the single amount that, if invested at the measurement date in a portfolio of high-quality debt instruments, would provide the necessary future cash flows to pay the accumulated benefits when due. Notionally, that single amount, the accumulated post retirement benefit obligation, would equal the current value of a portfolio of high-quality zero coupon bonds whose maturity*

39 W. Schuetze, "Letter from SEC to FASB Emerging Issues Task Force" (Sept. 22, 1993).

> *dates and amounts would be the same as the timing and amount of the expected future benefits payments.*[40]

FASB needs little or no translation here. Liabilities are to be priced as if they were zero coupon bonds whose maturities match the liability benefit dates and whose par values match the liability payment amounts. Since Treasuries are the dominant, if not only, zero coupon bonds with any sizable liquidity as a yield curve, it follows that **pension liabilities will behave like a portfolio of Treasury zero coupon bonds!** After decades of executing defeasance programs through the purchase of Treasury zero coupon bonds (i.e., pre-funding of municipal bonds), this should not be a surprise. By accounting definition, to *defease* liabilities, the purchased bond's future value must equal the liability's future value on the liability payment date(s). Therefore:

Pension Liabilities = Treasury Zero Coupon Bond Portfolio.

FAS No. 158 (now ASC 715)

In September 2006, FASB amended FAS No. 87, paragraph 44 as part of FAS No. 158 as follows:

> "n. Paragraph 44A is added as follows:
>
> Pursuant to paragraph 44, an employer may look to rates of return on high-quality fixed-income investments in determining assumed discount rates. The objective of selecting assumed discount rates using that method is to measure the single amount that, if invested at the measurement date in a portfolio of high-quality debt instruments, would provide the necessary fu-

40 FASB, Statement of Financial Accounting Standards No. 106 (Norwalk, CT: Financial Accounting Standards Board, 1986), par. 185.

> ture cash flows to pay the pension benefits when due. Notionally, that single amount, the projected benefit obligation, would equal the current market value of a portfolio of high-quality zero coupon bonds whose maturity dates and amounts would be the same as the timing and amount of the expected future benefit payments. Because cash inflows would equal cash outflows in timing and amount, there would be no reinvestment risk in the yields to maturity of the portfolio. However, in other than a zero coupon portfolio, such as a portfolio of long-term debt instruments that pay semiannual interest payments or whose maturities do not extend far enough into the future to meet expected benefit payments, the assumed discount rates (the yield to maturity) need to incorporate expected reinvestment rates available in the future. Those rates shall be extrapolated from the existing yield curve at the measurement date. The determination of the assumed discount rate is separate from the determination of the expected rate of return on plan assets whenever the actual portfolio differs from the hypothetical portfolio above. Assumed discount rates shall be reevaluated at each measurement date. If the general level of interest rates rises or declines, the assumed discount rates shall change in a similar manner."[41]

Apparently, FASB adopted the same language as FAS No. 106 for OPEB liabilities to apply to pensions as FAS No. 158. Such language clearly says the use of a zero coupon portfolio is the preferred discount rate methodology. However, FASB allowed for some discretion on the part of pension plan sponsors as far as whether to use a Trea-

41 FASB, Statement of Financial Accounting Standards No. 158, an amendment of FASB Statement No. 87, Par. 44 (Norwalk, CT: Financial Accounting Standards Board, Sept. 2006).

sury or a high quality (Aa) corporate bond zero coupon yield curve. But in the end, if market interest rates rise or decline, the assumed discount rates should follow in a similar manner.

Many companies took advantage of these relaxed FASB guidelines. They wanted the highest yields acceptable under FAS No. 158. Pension mathematical brains worked overtime to come up with a *bootstrapping* methodology using a cubic spline approach to produce an acceptable FAS No. 158 Aa corporate zero coupon bond discount rate yield curve. Currently, Citigroup and Ryan ALM seem to be the two leaders in providing such yield curve structures. FASB allows high-quality, zero coupon bonds to be any bonds with a rating of Aa or higher. Such a bootstrapping methodology is based on a yield curve of real corporate coupon bonds from which a zero coupon yield curve is extrapolated. Since zero coupon corporate bonds do not exist as a well-defined yield curve with any liquidity, we are dealing with *hypothetical* discount rates. The logic or strategy assumed by plan sponsors is that Aa corporate bonds have higher yields, which will equate to lower liability present values (e.g., 100 basis points lower discount rates = 10% lower liability valuation on a 10-year average duration; and 15% lower liability valuation on a 15-year average duration) which will lower contribution costs and possibly enhance the credit rating.

Shown in Exhibit 21 on the next page is the Ryan ALM version of FAS No. 158 (now ASC 715) pricing of a simple and linear liability benefit schedule of $20 million annually for 30 years ($600 million total future value) using both FAS No. 158 (AA corporate) and Treasury STRIPS (Exhibit 22) rates.

The major differences between the two pricing schemes should be quite clear. As of Dec. 31, 2012, the FAS No. 158 discount rate pricing has 82 basis points higher yields (2.744% vs. 1.925%) than Treasury STRIPS, thereby creating 12.87% lower present values and a 8.28% shorter modified duration given the same future value benefit

EXHIBIT 21

Ryan ALM Custom Liability Index
FAS 158 (ASC 715) - Structure
12/31/2012

Duration Cells	% Weight	# Payments	Future Value	Present Value	Coupon	Averages Price	YTW	MDUR
SHORT(0-1)	5.50	2	20,000,000	19,958,002	0.00	99.790	0.253	0.746
01.01 - 02.50	8.16	3	30,000,000	29,592,834	0.00	98.646	0.660	1.982
02.50 - 03.50	5.33	2	20,000,000	19,327,575	0.00	96.640	1.053	3.213
03.50 - 04.50	5.21	2	20,000,000	18,886,504	0.00	94.436	1.353	4.189
04.50 - 05.50	5.06	2	20,000,000	18,358,207	0.00	91.796	1.642	5.161
05.50 - 06.50	4.90	2	20,000,000	17,757,047	0.00	88.792	1.919	6.128
06.50 - 07.50	4.71	2	20,000,000	17,097,387	0.00	85.495	2.185	7.091
07.50 - 08.50	4.52	2	20,000,000	16,394,235	0.00	81.981	2.438	8.049
08.50 - 09.50	4.32	2	20,000,000	15,662,070	0.00	78.321	2.678	9.004
09.50 - 10.50	4.11	2	20,000,000	14,913,628	0.00	74.580	2.904	9.956
INTER(1- 10.50)	46.31	19	190,000,000	167,989,486	0.00	89.156	1.740	5.632
10.50 - 11.50	3.90	2	20,000,000	14,160,549	0.00	70.815	3.116	10.905
11.50 - 12.50	3.70	2	20,000,000	13,414,070	0.00	67.083	3.314	11.851
12.50 - 13.50	3.50	2	20,000,000	12,684,001	0.00	63.433	3.497	12.797
13.50 - 14.50	3.30	2	20,000,000	11,977,853	0.00	59.902	3.663	13.741
14.50 - 15.50	3.12	2	20,000,000	11,301,791	0.00	56.521	3.814	14.684
15.50 - 16.50	2.94	2	20,000,000	10,661,188	0.00	53.317	3.948	15.628
16.50 - 17.50	2.77	2	20,000,000	10,059,921	0.00	50.310	4.064	16.571
17.50 - 18.50	2.62	2	20,000,000	9,499,934	0.00	47.509	4.164	17.515
18.50 - 19.50	2.48	2	20,000,000	8,982,094	0.00	44.919	4.247	18.460
19.50 - 20.50	2.35	2	20,000,000	8,506,460	0.00	42.540	4.313	19.408
LONG(10.5 - 20.5)	30.67	20	200,000,000	111,247,861	0.00	57.122	3.751	14.714
20.50 - 21.51	2.23	2	20,000,000	8,071,923	0.00	40.366	4.363	20.356
21.50 - 22.50	2.12	2	20,000,000	7,676,124	0.00	38.386	4.398	21.308
22.50 - 23.50	2.02	2	20,000,000	7,315,956	0.00	36.585	4.421	22.261
23.50 - 24.50	1.93	2	20,000,000	6,987,581	0.00	34.942	4.433	23.216
24.50 - 25.50	1.84	2	20,000,000	6,686,349	0.00	33.436	4.435	24.173
25.50 - 26.50	1.77	2	20,000,000	6,406,898	0.00	32.038	4.433	25.132
26.50 - 27.50	1.69	2	20,000,000	6,143,275	0.00	30.720	4.427	26.091
27.50 - 28.50	1.62	2	20,000,000	5,888,901	0.00	29.448	4.424	27.049
28.50 - 29.50	1.55	2	20,000,000	5,636,658	0.00	28.187	4.425	28.006
29.50 - 30.50	0.75	1	10,000,000	2,722,339	0.00	27.223	4.432	28.727
VLONG(20.5+)	17.52	19	190,000,000	63,536,004	0.00	33.938	4.417	24.100
Total	100.00	60	600,000,000	362,731,353	0.00	70.244	2.744	11.383

EXHIBIT 22

Ryan ALM Custom Liability Index
TSY STRIP - Structure
12/31/2012

Duration Cells	% Weight	# Payments	Future Value	Present Value	Averages Coupon	Averages Price	Averages YTW	Averages MDUR
SHORT(0-1)	4.80	2	20,000,000	19,970,805	0.00	99.854	0.186	0.747
01.01 - 02.50	7.16	3	30,000,000	29,814,805	0.00	99.383	0.303	1.990
02.50 - 03.50	4.73	2	20,000,000	19,703,836	0.00	98.520	0.457	3.233
03.50 - 04.50	4.67	2	20,000,000	19,452,490	0.00	97.264	0.653	4.220
04.50 - 05.50	4.59	2	20,000,000	19,122,518	0.00	95.615	0.856	5.202
05.50 - 06.50	4.49	2	20,000,000	18,705,499	0.00	93.531	1.074	6.180
06.50 - 07.50	4.37	2	20,000,000	18,194,721	0.00	90.978	1.312	7.152
07.50 - 08.50	4.23	2	20,000,000	17,609,572	0.00	88.054	1.553	8.119
08.50 - 09.50	4.08	2	20,000,000	17,001,976	0.00	85.017	1.770	9.085
09.50 - 10.50	3.93	2	20,000,000	16,362,657	0.00	81.821	1.977	10.047
INTER(1- 10.50)	42.27	19	190,000,000	175,968,073	0.00	92.997	1.028	5.752
10.50 - 11.50	3.78	2	20,000,000	15,736,053	0.00	78.688	2.154	11.008
11.50 - 12.50	3.63	2	20,000,000	15,111,961	0.00	75.567	2.314	11.968
12.50 - 13.50	3.48	2	20,000,000	14,507,594	0.00	72.546	2.452	12.928
13.50 - 14.50	3.34	2	20,000,000	13,919,410	0.00	69.604	2.576	13.888
14.50 - 15.50	3.22	2	20,000,000	13,388,892	0.00	66.950	2.667	14.850
15.50 - 16.50	3.10	2	20,000,000	12,890,496	0.00	64.457	2.740	15.813
16.50 - 17.50	2.99	2	20,000,000	12,442,421	0.00	62.218	2.790	16.777
17.50 - 18.50	2.88	2	20,000,000	11,993,523	0.00	59.973	2.842	17.742
18.50 - 19.50	2.78	2	20,000,000	11,556,959	0.00	57.790	2.890	18.705
19.50 - 20.50	2.68	2	20,000,000	11,141,324	0.00	55.711	2.932	19.669
LONG(10.5 - 20.5)	31.87	20	200,000,000	132,688,633	0.00	67.156	2.609	15.031
20.50 - 21.51	2.58	2	20,000,000	10,738,156	0.00	53.696	2.970	20.633
21.50 - 22.50	2.48	2	20,000,000	10,344,171	0.00	51.725	3.008	21.596
22.50 - 23.50	2.40	2	20,000,000	10,009,291	0.00	50.051	3.022	22.564
23.50 - 24.50	2.31	2	20,000,000	9,628,506	0.00	48.147	3.061	23.526
24.50 - 25.50	2.23	2	20,000,000	9,271,996	0.00	46.364	3.092	24.489
25.50 - 26.50	2.14	2	20,000,000	8,919,792	0.00	44.603	3.124	25.450
26.50 - 27.50	2.07	2	20,000,000	8,596,877	0.00	42.987	3.147	26.415
27.50 - 28.50	1.99	2	20,000,000	8,291,869	0.00	41.463	3.166	27.379
28.50 - 29.50	1.92	2	20,000,000	7,981,363	0.00	39.909	3.191	28.342
29.50 - 30.50	0.94	1	10,000,000	3,897,402	0.00	38.974	3.191	29.072
VLONG(20.5+)	21.06	19	190,000,000	87,679,422	0.00	46.621	3.085	24.464
Total	100.00	60	600,000,000	416,306,932	0.00	75.322	1.925	12.410

schedule ($600 million). As a result, pricing liabilities off of market rates (Treasury STRIPS) will create greater interest rate sensitivity. FAS No. 158 will show higher growth rates in percent and dollars, but will still show lower ending present values than market rates per 100 basis points movement over a one-year horizon.

EXHIBIT 23

FAS NO. 158 VS. TREASURY STRIPS DISCOUNT RATES (12/31/12)

	FAS No. 158	Treasury STRIPS
Present Value (PV)	$362,731,353	$416,306,932
Yield to Maturity (YTM)	2.744%	1.925%
Modified Duration (yrs)	11.383	12.410
Interest Rate Sensitivity:		
+ 100 bps (return)	-6.83%	-9.28%
- 100 bps (return)	16.08%	15.55%
+ 100 bps (end PV)	$291,783,073	$359,560,865
- 100 bps (end PV)	$363,531,436	$457,958,334

"Common sense is not common ...
it requires Preferred sense."

—Ronald J. Ryan, CFA

CHAPTER **EIGHT**

"WOODY" THE PRIVATE PENSION PENCIL: PHANTOM EARNINGS

The pension asset is one of the largest assets of any corporation. The growth and behavior of pension assets have played major roles in the profitability of many corporations offering defined benefit plans. Since corporations are earnings-led and not liability-led, corporate executives have a mandate from their stockholders to act with prudence to enhance earnings and the stockholder value of the firm. There is nothing wrong with that objective. However, corporations have learned how pensions affect earnings, and more importantly, how to manipulate pensions to enhance earnings per share (EPS).

Pension benefits and contributions are major expenses for many corporations. Pensions are a cost factor, and as such, hurt earnings. However, FASB guidelines allow corporations to calculate pension cost in such a way that it could become pension income (credit) and actually enhance earnings. Net pension cost is generally made up of four main components: service cost, interest cost, expected return on plan assets (ROA), and amortization of unrecognized gains and losses. The primary reduction or offset to pension expense is the expected return on pension assets (ROA). When the dollar growth of pension assets exceeds pension expense, the result is pension income (credit), which enhances earnings. Pension expense, on the other hand, hurts earnings. The line items are as follows:

- **Service Cost:** The deferred compensation cost = the present value of the future retirement benefits that the employees earned by working during the current year.

- **Interest Cost:** Similar to the accretion on a zero coupon bond, this measures the increase in the pension obligation due to the passage of time.

- **Expected return on assets (ROA):** This is an estimate of what management expects to earn on the pension plan assets to reduce net pension cost. It is calculated by multiplying the expected rate of return on plan assets by the "market-related" value of plan assets. The market-related value can either be the fair value or a smoothed "calculated" value.

- **Amortization of unrecognized gains and losses** are due to smoothing mechanisms in FAS 87 and represent actual changes in the value of the pension obligation or plan assets that have not been recognized in earnings.[42] The actual growth of pension assets is compared to the ROA growth value. Any difference (gain/loss) is then amortized over the life of the pension active lives (at 10 to 15 years). This amortization is a direct hit to earnings. It is usually itemized as a line item titled "actuarial gain/loss". For example, an unrecognized loss will occur when the actual return on plan assets is less than the expected return (ROA). The unrecognized gains and losses can be amortized into earnings in a number of different ways. However, this minimum amortization must occur when the cumulative unrecognized gain or loss exceeds 10% of the market-related value of plan assets or the pension obligation, whichever is larger. The amount over this threshold is typically amortized over the

42 David Zion, Amit Varshney, Christopher Cornett, "FAS 87 . . . So Smooth," Credit Suisse First Boston (Nov. 11, 2008). www.credit-suisse.com.

remaining service life of the active employees. The minimum amortization is commonly referred to as the *corridor* approach. In the decade of the 2000s, most pension assets did not earn the ROA and have built up an amortized loss that will hurt earnings over a long period (remaining life of active employees = 10 to 15 years). The change in the liability discount rate is also another item here. If a discount rate change produces an actual liability growth different from the beginning of the year discount rate, such difference is amortized accordingly in the same way as assets. Before the unrecognized gain or loss is compared to the corridor, there is an additional step that many forget: the unrecognized gain or loss is adjusted for any unrecognized market-related gains or losses (i.e., the difference between the fair value of the plan assets and the market-related value). That adjustment is made only by companies using the calculated value method (as fair value and market-related value are the same under the fair value method), it's a hidden aspect of the smoothing, and it can have a significant impact on the amount amortized.[43]

The ROA is the major contra item to pension costs and is usually the major driver of turning pension expense into pension income. By raising the ROA, asset growth increases, thereby offsetting pension costs. Since pension expense is well-known a year in advance, corporations can figure out the ROA needed to wash out pension expense. But why stop there? All corporations need to do is just raise the ROA even higher to create pension income, or credit. Since the ROA has to be validated by auditors, the asset allocation model is put to the test of validating any ROA forecast. Although this may enhance earnings near term, such a procedure jeopardizes the health of pensions, causing pension plan sponsors to skew their asset allocation to riskier

43 David Zion, Amit Varshney, Christopher Cornett, "FAS 87 . . . So Smooth," Credit Suisse First Boston (Nov. 11, 2008). www.credit-suisse.com.

and riskier asset allocations to please the ROA validation. As funded ratios of pensions deteriorated in the decade of the 2000s, pension contributions grew, reducing, washing out or deteriorating any earnings value from the ROA manipulation.

Moreover, the amortization of unrecognized gains and losses (actuarial gain/loss) could be a plus or a minus to earnings. The actual return of pension assets is compared to the ROA forecast, and the actual growth of liabilities is compared to the discount rate used at the beginning of the fiscal year. The difference in asset growth, minus the difference in liability growth, minus a 10% corridor is then amortized over the average life of the employees' benefits for active lives (does not include retired lives). This amortization is either an actuarial gain or loss, which affects earnings accordingly. Since 1999, most corporate pension assets have had growth rates well *below* the ROA, and liability growth well *above* the beginning discount rate. This combination has resulted in significant actuarial losses. Such actuarial loss continues as a drag on earnings mainly due to the disastrous year of 2008. As shown in Exhibit 24 and presented in *The Ryan ALM Pension Letter*, my calculation of 2008 pension growth was about -24.47%. Compared to an ROA forecast of 8%, we see a -32.47% actuarial loss. Exhibit 24 (and *The Ryan ALM Pension Letter*) also show my calculation of 2008 liability growth under FAS No. 158 discount rates at 16.18%, versus a beginning discount rate of 5.913% for an actuarial loss of -10.27%. This adds up to an actuarial loss subtotal of -42.74%. We then subtract a corridor of either 10% of the assets or liabilities, whichever is larger. Assuming a funded ratio deficit of 20%, liabilities would be 25% higher than assets, equal to a corridor of 12.5%. Subtracting the subtotal actuarial loss of -42.74% by -12.50% gives an actuarial loss of -30.24%. This is then amortized over the average life of active employees at 10 to 15 years. **This becomes an annual hit or drag to earnings equal to -2.02% to -3.02% of pension assets for the next 10 to 15 years.** For most mature companies, 2% to 3% of pension assets as an actuarial loss would be a serious dilution of EPS.

EXHIBIT 24

2008 ACTUARIAL LOSS	
Actual Return on Assets	-24.47%
- Forecasted ROA	8.00%
Difference (Actuarial Loss)	-32.47%
Actual Growth of Liabilities (FAS No. 158)	16.18%
- Discount Rate	5.91%
Difference (Actuarial Loss)	10.27%
Subtotal Actuarial Loss (Assets + Liabilities)	-42.74%
- Corridor	12.5%
Actuarial Loss	**-30.24%**
Amortization (Average Life of Active Lives)	10 to 15 years
Actuarial Loss per year	**-2.02% to -3.02%**

Lucent Technology

Perhaps the most acute example of pensions being used to enhance earnings was Lucent Technology. Lucent was merged into Alcatel in 2006, but prior to that time, it consistently showed pension income or pension credit as a sizable contributor to net income (55% to 100% from 2003 to 2005). While most corporations were using an ROA of 8% or lower, Lucent Technology raised their ROA to 8.75% (2003), 8.75% (2004), and 8.50% (2005). The higher the ROA, the more net pension costs are reduced until they become a credit (pension income) and enhance earnings, as Exhibit 25 below illustrates.

EXHIBIT 25

HISTORY OF LUCENT TECHNOLOGY NET INCOME[3]

	2003	2004	2005
Net Income ($ millions)	$1,185	$2,002	$ (770)
Pension Credit	973	1,111	1,097
Pension Credit/Net Income	82%	55%	100% +

One would think that the *quality* of Lucent Technology's reported earnings would be judged as poor or suspect, yet it tends to be a prevalent trend in America. The fact remains that few security analysts consider pensions when analyzing corporate stocks and bonds. I would like to congratulate Credit Suisse for its thorough watchdog approach with respect to how pensions affect corporate financial statements.

Smoothing Assets (Calculated Value)

FAS No. 87 allows corporations to *smooth* pension assets. Such a rule was created to reduce reported earnings volatility. One can only assume that corporations lobbied heavily for such a ruling. FAS No. 87 provides asset valuation options. Corporations have the choice of using market-related value (also known as fair value) or a smoothed calculated value on pension assets. Smoothing can be used over various periods not to exceed five years. Whatever valuation is chosen, a return on asset (ROA) assumption is then applied. In a down market (i.e., 2000-2002, 2008) companies using the market value (fair value) of plan assets will be applying expected rates of return to lower asset

44 Lucent Technologies Inc., *2003, 2004*, and *2005 Annual Reports.*

bases, resulting in lower expected dollar return on plan assets, higher pension costs, and lower earnings. The exact opposite would take place when the plan assets are performing well (i.e., decade of the 1990s). Companies using the fair value method will see more volatile pension costs that will move inversely and directly with the plan assets (when assets go up, pension costs go down, and vice versa), while companies that use calculated value (smoothing) will see less volatile pension costs that may not move in sync with the plan assets and will report a more unrealistic funded ratio.[45]

The method by which a company determines the value of pension assets can have a significant impact on pension costs reported in earnings. Let's start with the impact from the expected return on assets (ROA): Applying the same forecasted rate of return (ROA) to a different asset base will yield a different expected dollar return on plan assets. In addition, the method for determining the valuation of pension assets will also affect another component of pension cost: the *amortization of unrecognized gains and losses.* Many companies amortize the minimum amount that's determined by comparing the cumulative unrecognized gain or loss to the corridor. Gains or losses in excess of the corridor are amortized over the remaining service life of the employees. The corridor is either 10% of the market-related value of plan assets, or 10% of the projected benefit obligation (PBO liabilities), whichever is larger. Therefore, how the market-related value of plan assets is determined can impact the corridor, which can affect the amount of unrecognized gains and losses that are amortized.

---

45 David Zion, Amit Varshney, Christopher Cornett, "FAS 87 . . . So Smooth," Credit Suisse First Boston (Nov. 11, 2008). www.credit-suisse.com.

Fair Value vs. Calculated Value[46]

The companies that use fair value (market value) for determining the market-related value of plan assets should have more volatile pension costs than those using smoothing or calculated value. The accounting can show dramatically different results, even though the economics of the pension plan may be exactly the same as another company that is using calculated value. With plan assets dropping so significantly in 2008, the companies using the fair value method probably wouldn't mind switching to using calculated values. However, for a company to make a change in accounting method, it must justify that it is making a change to a preferable method. Why might calculated value be a preferable method right now? Perhaps because it increases earnings and reduces earnings volatility! It is unlikely that auditors or the SEC would accept the argument that calculated value is a preferable method since calculated value does such a poor job of reflecting what is really happening to the pension plan when determining pension costs. If you are a security analyst or investor focused on earnings, you might be interested in knowing which of these methods a company is using; one problem: most companies won't tell you. Of the 371 companies in the S&P 500 with a pension plan, Credit Suisse found that only 105 of them disclose which method they are using: 17 use fair value, and 88 use calculated value.

Exhibit 26 on the following page shows that the method selected to value pension assets can have a significant effect on pension costs and EPS. In the companies listed, all those switching from fair value to calculated value following 2008's disastrous pension asset performance reduced pension costs and enhanced 2009 EPS as shown. Only Aon switched from calculated value to fair value, which cost them $(0.56) EPS due to increased pension costs.

---

46 David Zion, Amit Varshney, Christopher Cornett, "FAS 87 . . . So Smooth," Credit Suisse First Boston (Nov. 11, 2008). www.credit-suisse.com.

EXHIBIT 26

EPS EFFECT OF CHANGING MARKET-RELATED VALUE OF PLAN ASSETS ON ESTIMATED 2009

	Old Method	Pension Cost	New Method	Pension Cost	Cost Difference
FedEx	FV	$1.60	CV	$0.42	$(1.17)
Aon Corp.	CV	0.18	FV	0.74	0.56
DTE Energy	FV	0.65	CV	0.17	(0.48)
Exelon	FV	0.51	CV	0.09	(0.41)
Air Products	FV	0.45	CV	0.13	(0.32)
Rockwell Collins	FV	0.27	CV	(0.05)	(0.32)
Hartford Financial	FV	0.36	CV	0.08	(0.28)
Pitney-Bowes	FV	0.27	CV	0.02	(0.26)

FV = Fair Value, CV = Calculated Value (Smoothing)

Source: Credit Suisse

"This is one of those cases in which the imagination is baffled by the facts."

—Adam Smith

CHAPTER **NINE**

"WOODY" THE PRIVATE PENSION PENCIL: GM: PENSION OBLIGATION BONDS

By 2002, GM had an unfunded pension liability estimated at $19.3 billion,[47] which was larger than its net worth of $7 billion. What to do? GM could either go bankrupt or figure out some creative financing. Apparently, GM called in Woody, the magic pension accounting pencil, to ask for some advice. Woody said, "Issue pension obligation bonds!" The accounting benefits of this strategy may amaze you.

First, interest expense is a tax deduction item so issuing corporate debt is not as expensive as one might think: debt issuance yield - corporate tax rate of 35% = net interest expense. Second, pension contributions are a tax credit, so raising funds through a pension obligation bond (POB) can be transferred over to pensions as a contribution with a one-time tax advantage or deduction. This transfer would also shore up pensions, reducing or eliminating contribution costs as the funded ratio is enhanced, which would also enhance the creditworthiness of GM. Third, pensions are tax-exempt entities, so the pension assets grow without any tax dilution. This favorable tax treatment plays a role in earnings (pension expense/income calculation). Fourth, FASB

47 G. Bennett Steward III, "Pension Roulette: Have You Bet Too Much on Equities?" *Harvard Business Review* 81, no. 6 (June 2003): 104-110. http://hbr.org/2003/06/pension-roulette-have-you-bet-too-much-on-equities/ar/1.

allows pension asset returns (ROA) to be forecasted! As a result, a sensational arbitrage between the ROA and net interest cost can be created. Any positive difference goes directly to EPS as pension income (i.e., credit). Alas, based on Woody's advice, GM proceeded to issue a series of pension obligation bonds (POBs) in July 2003 (see Exhibit 27).

EXHIBIT 27

GM'S ISSUANCE OF PENSION OBLIGATION BONDS (ESTIMATED)

Type	Par Value	Coupon	Maturity
Convertible	$4.3 billion	6.25%	July 15, 2033
Senior Notes	$1.0 billion	7.125%	July 15, 2033
	$1.25 billion	8.25%	July 15, 2013
	$3.0 billion	8.375%	July 15, 2013
Euro-Denominated Senior Notes			
	$1.0 billion	7.25%	July 3, 2013
	$1.5 billion	8.375%	July 15, 2033
Pound-Sterling Denominated Notes			
	$0.35 billion	8.375%	December 7, 2015
	$0.25 billion	8.875%	July 10, 2023
Total	**$13 billion**	**7.859% (estimated)**	

EXHIBIT 28

ESTIMATED ANNUAL FINANCIAL IMPACT FROM GM ISSUANCE OF POBS

	Corporate	Pension Fund
(Debt) / Contribution	($13,000,000,000)	$13,000,000,000
35% Tax Credit	$ 4,550,000,000	
Annual Interest	$ 1,021,670,000	
35% Tax Deduction	$ 357,584,500	
Net Interest Cost	$ 664,085,500	
ROA of Pension (9.00%)		$ 1,170,000,000
PHANTOM Earnings	$ 505,914,500 (annually)	ROA = Net Interest Cost

As Exhibit 28 illustrates, GM issued approximately $13 billion in POBs at an average interest rate of 7.859%. After a 35% tax rate assumption, the net interest cost is 5.108%. Proceeds were added to the pension as a contribution, and GM received a one-time tax credit of approximately $4.55 billion. GM then assumed a **9% ROA** (high estimate) on the pension assets, which grow tax free. A 9% growth rate on assets minus a 5.108% cost factor creates an arbitrage equal to 3.891% on $13 billion, which equals $505.9 million *phantom earnings* annually over the maturity of the bonds. By issuing the POBs, GM was also able to enhance the funded ratio of the pension to an adequate level, thereby reducing or eliminating future contribution costs —*Bravo*, Woody!

Note that the ROA is a forecast of pension asset growth. The actual growth is compared to the ROA (minus a 10% corridor) that is amortized over the average life of active employees (10 to 15 years). This becomes a direct hit to EPS as an actuarial gain or loss. Good luck to GM earning 9.00% on pension assets.

GM was investigated for its pension accounting, as well as for transactions with bankrupt auto-parts maker Delphi Corporation. The SEC has investigated a series of companies, studying whether they inflated profits or minimized earnings swings by using unreasonable assumptions in order to value pension assets and liabilities. In the last several years, the SEC has also reviewed Boeing Co., Northwest Airlines Inc., Navistar International Corp., Sysco Corp., and Walt Disney Co. So far they all were found to be in compliance with FASB accounting rules—and that is the true villain of our story. FASB allows a company to assume a static positive annual return on pension fund assets such as stocks, even if the assets lost value that year (as they did in 2008).

The SEC's probes of GM included: financial reporting of pension and other retiree benefit programs; transactions between the automaker and Delphi; recovery of recall costs from suppliers and supplier price reductions and credits; and GM's possible obligation to fund Delphi's pensions. During such probes, the SEC asks company representatives to be as specific as possible in disclosing the assumptions they use to calculate pension costs and asset returns. In a letter to Caterpillar Inc. in June 2003, SEC staff encouraged the company to include previous years' pension returns in calculating its future retirement costs.

On the one hand, GM's management should have been congratulated on their focus and attention to their pension dilemma and their creative financial solutions. However, new areas of concern were raised that may have been fatal to GM's existence:

1. Leverage

The pension deficit reduction of $13 billion (which represents about 67% of the $19.3 billion GM pension deficit) was a result of issuing pension obligation bonds. This means a shifting of liabilities from the pension to the corporate side. This debt also has to be paid over a shorter period than the pension schedule. GM's capital structure now has more leverage with a debt increase of about 7%.

2. Earnings Drag (Actuarial Loss)

GM was carrying a very large amortized actuarial loss from the 2000 to 2002 pension asset disaster years, due to underperforming a 10% ROA. This actuarial loss rose from $730 million in 2002 to $1.744 billion in 2003.[48] Such an actuarial loss of about $1.7 billion would be amortized for another 5+ years. Although the ROA forecast was lowered to 9% in 2003, the years 2003 to 2008 apparently did not improve the actuarial loss situation. As a result, the ROA underperformance created a sizable EPS drag on future earnings that even the POB arbitrage couldn't erase. In fact, adding $13 billion more pension assets might create a larger actuarial loss. Every 1% underperformance versus the 9% ROA would result in about a $130 million

48 General Motors Cooperation, *Annual Report 2003.*

actuarial loss amortized over 10 to 15 years. Moreover, lowering the ROA from 10% to 9% increased pension expense, which is another hit to earnings.

3. Pension Obligation Bonds (POBs)

The POB issuance has interest costs of approximately $1 billion per year plus principal payments of $13 billion that hurt the income statement and balance sheet. It is new debt.

4. Discount Rate

The discount rate used to price pension liabilities was lowered from 6.75% to 6.00% in conformity with FAS No. 158. This raised the present value of liabilities (PBO) from $79.6 billion (2002) to $87.3 billion (2003).[49]

"Hakuna matata." (No worries).

—*The Lion King*

49 Ibid.

CHAPTER TEN

"WOODY" THE PRIVATE PENSION PENCIL: PENSION PROTECTION ACT (PPA)

After the defined benefit pension debacle of 2000-2002 during which funded ratios fell by 30% to 60%, Congress passed the Pension Protection Act (PPA) that was signed into law Aug. 17, 2006, by Pres. Bush to help shore up America's pension system. The PPA is, by far, the most comprehensive pension reform since ERISA was passed in 1974. The PPA revised funding rules that dictate the minimum and maximum required contribution. This pension reform act requires corporate pension plans to fully fund their liabilities within the next seven years from enactment of the PPA. For most plans, PPA's funding rules took effect with the 2008 pension plan year.

Funding Target

The funding target, or funded ratio, is defined as the ratio of the market value of pension assets divided by the present value of a plan's accrued benefits (and is akin to "current liability" under pre-PPA law). The relationship between a plan's liabilities and its assets determines the plan's minimum and maximum required contributions, PBGC premiums, and benefit payment restrictions.[50] The PPA increased the funding ratio target for single employer defined benefit pension plans from 90% (pre-PPA) to 100%. If a plan meets its funding ratio target as of the beginning of the plan year, the employer's minimum required contribution for that year equals its target normal cost with no extra contribution. A plan's target normal cost is the present value of benefit liabilities expected to accrue during the year, including increases in benefits earned over prior years as a result of salary increases. If a plan's funded status exceeds 100%, the surplus of plan assets over liabilities reduces the employer's minimum required contribution for the year. When a plan is less than 100% funded, the plan sponsor must make contributions (in addition to the target normal cost) to amortize the shortfall. Each plan year that a plan fails to meet its funding target, the plan adds a new shortfall that must be amortized over seven years. The minimum required contribution for that plan year equals the plan's normal cost plus the amount required to amortize the shortfall for that year and every year after 2008 up to a total amortization period of seven years. Once a plan is 100% funded, all prior shortfall amortization bases are eliminated.[51]

Credit Balances

A credit balance occurs when a plan sponsor makes contributions in excess of the minimum required contribution for any given year. Under the PPA, this credit balance can be used to either (1) reduce the minimum required contribution for that year, or (2) increase the value of the assets in determining the funded ratio. The credit balance is thereby reduced and cannot be used again. If there is a credit

50 Buck Consultants, LLC, "IRS Issues on PPA Funding Rules for Single-Employer Defined Benefit Plans," *Buck Research* 31, iss. 05 (Jan. 11, 2008). http://www.buckconsultants.com/portals/0/publications/FYI/2008/FYI_01_11_08a.pdf.

51 HayGroup, *The Pension Protection Act of 2006: Summary of Multiemployer Defined Benefit Plan Provisions (Philadelphia, PA: Hay Acquisition* (Hay Acquisition Company I, Inc., Nov. 2006). http://www.haygroup.com/downloads/us/Hay_Group_PPA_2006_-_Multiemployer_Provisions.pdf.

balance at the end of plan year 2007, it is carried forward and added in. The credit balance is adjusted annually by the real rate of return on the plan assets.

Discount Rates

The PPA offers basically two alternatives to discounting pension liabilities: (1) a "spot rate" full yield curve and (2) a "three segment rates" yield curve defined as maturities between 0 to five years, five to 20 years, and over 20 years. The three segment rates yield curve is also an average discount rate over the last 25 years, and the average can be based on annual, semi-annual, quarterly, or monthly fair market values. The method chosen will determine the funding target and target normal cost. Such PPA discount rates are high-quality *zero coupon* corporate bond rates provided monthly by the Treasury Department. Interestingly, the discount rates published by the Treasury are based on monthly averages with a one-month lag. As a result, the November discount rates are based on a monthly average of rates for October (spot rate yield curve) or a monthly average of the last 25 years ending in October (three segment yield curve).

These discount rates are in sharp contrast to the previous discount rates required for funding purposes under the IRS code, which were 30-year Treasury rates and a 24-month average. The revised PPA rates are higher yielding and therefore, all things being equal, would produce a lower liability valuation, a higher funded ratio, and lower contribution costs.

Unfortunately, we are once again dealing with discount rate magic and "believe it or not" situations. First, we are using hypothetical bonds that do not exist. Zero-coupon corporate bonds are a rarity, especially as a yield curve. Second, we have a moving average (or smoothing methodology) that by definition can never represent current fair market values for liabilities, which distorts the funded ratio (either overvaluing or undervaluing it) and affects the minimum required contribution. Third, the discount rates are monthly averages. Add it up, and you get quite an ambrosia of valuations. It might taste good, but it is certainly not accurate.

In an effort to inform plan sponsors of an accurate and frequent calculation of the valuation and growth rate differences of their liabilities, Ryan ALM provides a custom liability index (CLI) as monthly structure, performance, and interest rate sensitivity reports based on each client's actuarial projections of their benefit payment schedule. The Ryan ALM Custom Liability Index is a series of monthly reports wherein liabilities are priced at every discount rate methodology, including: FAS 158 (now ASC 715), PPA (MAP-21 three segment rates), PPA spot rates, GASB, plus market rates (U.S. Treasury STRIPS yield curve). The differences in discount rate pricing between the FAS 158, PPA (MAP-21), PPA spot rates, GASB, and market rates can be quite significant. This could misvalue the funded ratio, which would misinform and misdirect asset allocation decisions, benefit decisions, and contribution decisions... it all links!

Exhibits 29 through 32, shown on the next few pages, present the Ryan ALM Custom Liability Index structure report, which calculates the present value of liabilities, yield-to-worst (YTW), and modified duration as a term structure showing not only total averages but precise calculations for each annual year of liabilities (either as annual duration cells or annual fiscal years). Exhibits 29 through 32 are based on a generic custom liability index using a linear liability benefits schedule of $20 million per year for 30 years ($600 million future value).

EXHIBIT 29

Ryan ALM Custom Liability Index
TSY STRIP - Structure
12/31/2012

Duration Cells	% Weight	# Payments	Future Value	Present Value	Averages Coupon	Price	YTW	MDUR
SHORT(0-1)	4.80	2	20,000,000	19,970,805	0.00	99.854	0.186	0.747
01.01 - 02.50	7.16	3	30,000,000	29,814,805	0.00	99.383	0.303	1.990
02.50 - 03.50	4.73	2	20,000,000	19,703,836	0.00	98.520	0.457	3.233
03.50 - 04.50	4.67	2	20,000,000	19,452,490	0.00	97.264	0.653	4.220
04.50 - 05.50	4.59	2	20,000,000	19,122,518	0.00	95.615	0.856	5.202
05.50 - 06.50	4.49	2	20,000,000	18,705,499	0.00	93.531	1.074	6.180
06.50 - 07.50	4.37	2	20,000,000	18,194,721	0.00	90.978	1.312	7.152
07.50 - 08.50	4.23	2	20,000,000	17,609,572	0.00	88.054	1.553	8.119
08.50 - 09.50	4.08	2	20,000,000	17,001,976	0.00	85.017	1.770	9.085
09.50 - 10.50	3.93	2	20,000,000	16,362,657	0.00	81.821	1.977	10.047
INTER(1- 10.50)	42.27	19	190,000,000	175,968,073	0.00	92.997	1.028	5.752
10.50 - 11.50	3.78	2	20,000,000	15,736,053	0.00	78.688	2.154	11.008
11.50 - 12.50	3.63	2	20,000,000	15,111,961	0.00	75.567	2.314	11.968
12.50 - 13.50	3.48	2	20,000,000	14,507,594	0.00	72.546	2.452	12.928
13.50 - 14.50	3.34	2	20,000,000	13,919,410	0.00	69.604	2.576	13.888
14.50 - 15.50	3.22	2	20,000,000	13,388,892	0.00	66.950	2.667	14.850
15.50 - 16.50	3.10	2	20,000,000	12,890,496	0.00	64.457	2.740	15.813
16.50 - 17.50	2.99	2	20,000,000	12,442,421	0.00	62.218	2.790	16.777
17.50 - 18.50	2.88	2	20,000,000	11,993,523	0.00	59.973	2.842	17.742
18.50 - 19.50	2.78	2	20,000,000	11,556,959	0.00	57.790	2.890	18.705
19.50 - 20.50	2.68	2	20,000,000	11,141,324	0.00	55.711	2.932	19.669
LONG(10.5 - 20.5)	31.87	20	200,000,000	132,688,633	0.00	67.156	2.609	15.031
20.50 - 21.51	2.58	2	20,000,000	10,738,156	0.00	53.696	2.970	20.633
21.50 - 22.50	2.48	2	20,000,000	10,344,171	0.00	51.725	3.008	21.596
22.50 - 23.50	2.40	2	20,000,000	10,009,291	0.00	50.051	3.022	22.564
23.50 - 24.50	2.31	2	20,000,000	9,628,506	0.00	48.147	3.061	23.526
24.50 - 25.50	2.23	2	20,000,000	9,271,996	0.00	46.364	3.092	24.489
25.50 - 26.50	2.14	2	20,000,000	8,919,792	0.00	44.603	3.124	25.450
26.50 - 27.50	2.07	2	20,000,000	8,596,877	0.00	42.987	3.147	26.415
27.50 - 28.50	1.99	2	20,000,000	8,291,869	0.00	41.463	3.166	27.379
28.50 - 29.50	1.92	2	20,000,000	7,981,363	0.00	39.909	3.191	28.342
29.50 - 30.50	0.94	1	10,000,000	3,897,402	0.00	38.974	3.191	29.072
VLONG(20.5+)	21.06	19	190,000,000	87,679,422	0.00	46.621	3.085	24.464
Total	100.00	60	600,000,000	416,306,932	0.00	75.322	1.925	12.410

EXHIBIT 30

Ryan ALM Custom Liability Index
FAS 158 (ASC 715) - Structure
12/31/2012

Duration Cells	% Weight	# Payments	Future Value	Present Value	Coupon	Averages Price	YTW	MDUR
SHORT(0-1)	5.50	2	20,000,000	19,958,002	0.00	99.790	0.253	0.746
01.01 - 02.50	8.16	3	30,000,000	29,592,834	0.00	98.646	0.660	1.982
02.50 - 03.50	5.33	2	20,000,000	19,327,575	0.00	96.640	1.053	3.213
03.50 - 04.50	5.21	2	20,000,000	18,886,504	0.00	94.436	1.353	4.189
04.50 - 05.50	5.06	2	20,000,000	18,358,207	0.00	91.796	1.642	5.161
05.50 - 06.50	4.90	2	20,000,000	17,757,047	0.00	88.792	1.919	6.128
06.50 - 07.50	4.71	2	20,000,000	17,097,387	0.00	85.495	2.185	7.091
07.50 - 08.50	4.52	2	20,000,000	16,394,235	0.00	81.981	2.438	8.049
08.50 - 09.50	4.32	2	20,000,000	15,662,070	0.00	78.321	2.678	9.004
09.50 - 10.50	4.11	2	20,000,000	14,913,628	0.00	74.580	2.904	9.956
INTER(1- 10.50)	46.31	19	190,000,000	167,989,486	0.00	89.156	1.740	5.632
10.50 - 11.50	3.90	2	20,000,000	14,160,549	0.00	70.815	3.116	10.905
11.50 - 12.50	3.70	2	20,000,000	13,414,070	0.00	67.083	3.314	11.851
12.50 - 13.50	3.50	2	20,000,000	12,684,001	0.00	63.433	3.497	12.797
13.50 - 14.50	3.30	2	20,000,000	11,977,853	0.00	59.902	3.663	13.741
14.50 - 15.50	3.12	2	20,000,000	11,301,791	0.00	56.521	3.814	14.684
15.50 - 16.50	2.94	2	20,000,000	10,661,188	0.00	53.317	3.948	15.628
16.50 - 17.50	2.77	2	20,000,000	10,059,921	0.00	50.310	4.064	16.571
17.50 - 18.50	2.62	2	20,000,000	9,499,934	0.00	47.509	4.164	17.515
18.50 - 19.50	2.48	2	20,000,000	8,982,094	0.00	44.919	4.247	18.460
19.50 - 20.50	2.35	2	20,000,000	8,506,460	0.00	42.540	4.313	19.408
LONG(10.5 - 20.5)	30.67	20	200,000,000	111,247,861	0.00	57.122	3.751	14.714
20.50 - 21.51	2.23	2	20,000,000	8,071,923	0.00	40.366	4.363	20.356
21.50 - 22.50	2.12	2	20,000,000	7,676,124	0.00	38.386	4.398	21.308
22.50 - 23.50	2.02	2	20,000,000	7,315,956	0.00	36.585	4.421	22.261
23.50 - 24.50	1.93	2	20,000,000	6,987,581	0.00	34.942	4.433	23.216
24.50 - 25.50	1.84	2	20,000,000	6,686,349	0.00	33.436	4.435	24.173
25.50 - 26.50	1.77	2	20,000,000	6,406,898	0.00	32.038	4.433	25.132
26.50 - 27.50	1.69	2	20,000,000	6,143,275	0.00	30.720	4.427	26.091
27.50 - 28.50	1.62	2	20,000,000	5,888,901	0.00	29.448	4.424	27.049
28.50 - 29.50	1.55	2	20,000,000	5,636,658	0.00	28.187	4.425	28.006
29.50 - 30.50	0.75	1	10,000,000	2,722,339	0.00	27.223	4.432	28.727
VLONG(20.5+)	17.52	19	190,000,000	63,536,004	0.00	33.938	4.417	24.100
Total	100.00	60	600,000,000	362,731,353	0.00	70.244	2.744	11.383

EXHIBIT 31

Ryan ALM Custom Liability Index
IRS PPA (Spot Rates) - Structure
12/31/2012

Duration Cells	% Weight	# Payments	Future Value	Present Value	Averages Coupon	Price	YTW	MDUR
SHORT(0-1)	5.59	2	20,000,000	19,932,426	0.00	99.662	0.420	0.745
01.01 - 02.50	8.27	3	30,000,000	29,497,497	0.00	98.328	0.829	1.978
02.50 - 03.50	5.41	2	20,000,000	19,303,055	0.00	96.517	1.095	3.211
03.50 - 04.50	5.30	2	20,000,000	18,921,713	0.00	94.612	1.310	4.192
04.50 - 05.50	5.16	2	20,000,000	18,407,811	0.00	92.045	1.590	5.164
05.50 - 06.50	4.97	2	20,000,000	17,745,254	0.00	88.736	1.929	6.127
06.50 - 07.50	4.75	2	20,000,000	16,963,556	0.00	84.831	2.295	7.082
07.50 - 08.50	4.51	2	20,000,000	16,102,725	0.00	80.529	2.660	8.030
08.50 - 09.50	4.27	2	20,000,000	15,227,332	0.00	76.153	2.990	8.976
09.50 - 10.50	4.03	2	20,000,000	14,365,777	0.00	71.845	3.280	9.919
INTER(1- 10.50)	46.67	19	190,000,000	166,534,720	0.00	88.571	1.851	5.597
10.50 - 11.50	3.80	2	20,000,000	13,543,840	0.00	67.734	3.525	10.861
11.50 - 12.50	3.58	2	20,000,000	12,762,091	0.00	63.824	3.735	11.804
12.50 - 13.50	3.38	2	20,000,000	12,054,406	0.00	60.284	3.895	12.748
13.50 - 14.50	3.20	2	20,000,000	11,413,608	0.00	57.078	4.015	13.695
14.50 - 15.50	3.03	2	20,000,000	10,821,401	0.00	54.116	4.110	14.643
15.50 - 16.50	2.88	2	20,000,000	10,273,408	0.00	51.375	4.185	15.592
16.50 - 17.50	2.74	2	20,000,000	9,771,669	0.00	48.865	4.240	16.544
17.50 - 18.50	2.61	2	20,000,000	9,308,794	0.00	46.551	4.280	17.496
18.50 - 19.50	2.48	2	20,000,000	8,861,135	0.00	44.312	4.320	18.448
19.50 - 20.50	2.37	2	20,000,000	8,453,201	0.00	42.272	4.345	19.402
LONG(10.5 - 20.5)	30.06	20	200,000,000	107,263,552	0.00	54.858	4.027	14.715
20.50 - 21.51	2.26	2	20,000,000	8,059,843	0.00	40.306	4.370	20.356
21.50 - 22.50	2.15	2	20,000,000	7,681,696	0.00	38.414	4.395	21.309
22.50 - 23.50	2.06	2	20,000,000	7,341,727	0.00	36.714	4.405	22.264
23.50 - 24.50	1.96	2	20,000,000	6,999,330	0.00	35.002	4.425	23.218
24.50 - 25.50	1.87	2	20,000,000	6,670,393	0.00	33.357	4.445	24.171
25.50 - 26.50	1.78	2	20,000,000	6,362,721	0.00	31.817	4.460	25.125
26.50 - 27.50	1.70	2	20,000,000	6,066,986	0.00	30.339	4.475	26.078
27.50 - 28.50	1.62	2	20,000,000	5,775,983	0.00	28.884	4.495	27.030
28.50 - 29.50	1.54	2	20,000,000	5,511,835	0.00	27.563	4.505	27.984
29.50 - 30.50	0.74	1	10,000,000	2,654,423	0.00	26.544	4.520	28.703
VLONG(20.5+)	17.69	19	190,000,000	63,124,938	0.00	33.785	4.440	24.073
Total	100.00	60	600,000,000	356,855,635	0.00	69.366	2.883	11.335

EXHIBIT 32

Ryan ALM Custom Liability Index
IRS PPA (MAP 21) - Structure
12/31/2012

Duration Cells	% Weight	# Payments	Future Value	Present Value	Coupon	Averages Price	YTW	MDUR
SHORT(0-1)	7.08	2	20,000,000	19,290,142	0.00	96.465	4.940	0.716
01.01 - 02.50	10.00	3	30,000,000	27,250,888	0.00	90.871	4.940	1.895
02.50 - 03.50	6.28	2	20,000,000	17,101,949	0.00	85.522	4.940	3.092
03.50 - 04.50	5.98	2	20,000,000	16,296,883	0.00	81.496	4.940	4.045
04.50 - 05.50	5.70	2	20,000,000	15,529,715	0.00	77.660	4.940	4.998
05.50 - 06.50	5.05	2	20,000,000	13,776,244	0.00	68.896	6.150	5.883
06.50 - 07.50	4.76	2	20,000,000	12,978,091	0.00	64.905	6.150	6.825
07.50 - 08.50	4.49	2	20,000,000	12,226,181	0.00	61.144	6.150	7.767
08.50 - 09.50	4.23	2	20,000,000	11,517,834	0.00	57.602	6.150	8.709
09.50 - 10.50	3.98	2	20,000,000	10,850,527	0.00	54.265	6.150	9.651
INTER(1- 10.50)	50.46	19	190,000,000	137,528,313	0.00	74.635	5.480	5.218
10.50 - 11.50	3.75	2	20,000,000	10,221,881	0.00	51.121	6.150	10.593
11.50 - 12.50	3.53	2	20,000,000	9,629,657	0.00	48.159	6.150	11.535
12.50 - 13.50	3.33	2	20,000,000	9,071,745	0.00	45.369	6.150	12.477
13.50 - 14.50	3.14	2	20,000,000	8,546,156	0.00	42.740	6.150	13.419
14.50 - 15.50	2.95	2	20,000,000	8,051,019	0.00	40.264	6.150	14.361
15.50 - 16.50	2.78	2	20,000,000	7,584,568	0.00	37.931	6.150	15.303
16.50 - 17.50	2.62	2	20,000,000	7,145,141	0.00	35.734	6.150	16.245
17.50 - 18.50	2.47	2	20,000,000	6,731,174	0.00	33.663	6.150	17.187
18.50 - 19.50	2.33	2	20,000,000	6,341,191	0.00	31.713	6.150	18.129
19.50 - 20.50	2.19	2	20,000,000	5,973,802	0.00	29.876	6.150	19.071
LONG(10.5 - 20.5)	29.10	20	200,000,000	79,296,334	0.00	40.815	6.150	14.371
20.50 - 21.51	1.83	2	20,000,000	4,982,686	0.00	24.920	6.760	19.899
21.50 - 22.50	1.71	2	20,000,000	4,667,184	0.00	23.342	6.760	20.835
22.50 - 23.50	1.60	2	20,000,000	4,371,660	0.00	21.864	6.760	21.772
23.50 - 24.50	1.50	2	20,000,000	4,094,848	0.00	20.480	6.760	22.709
24.50 - 25.50	1.41	2	20,000,000	3,835,564	0.00	19.183	6.760	23.646
25.50 - 26.50	1.32	2	20,000,000	3,592,698	0.00	17.968	6.760	24.582
26.50 - 27.50	1.23	2	20,000,000	3,365,209	0.00	16.830	6.760	25.519
27.50 - 28.50	1.16	2	20,000,000	3,152,126	0.00	15.765	6.760	26.456
28.50 - 29.50	1.08	2	20,000,000	2,952,534	0.00	14.767	6.760	27.392
29.50 - 30.50	0.52	1	10,000,000	1,405,216	0.00	14.052	6.760	28.100
VLONG(20.5+)	13.36	19	190,000,000	36,419,724	0.00	19.779	6.760	23.427
Total	100.00	60	600,000,000	272,534,513	0.00	59.009	5.808	9.996

As shown in Exhibits 29 to 32, there are significant differences in all of the critical data calculations as follows:

EXHIBIT 33

12/31/12 DISCOUNT RATE DIFFERENCES (TREASURY VS. PPA) – $ MILLIONS						
	PV	**YTW**	**MDur**	**PV**	**YTW**	**MDur**
STRIPS	$416.3	1.926%	12.410			
PPA (3 Segment)	$254.3	6.447%	9.536	-38.91%	334.74%	-23.16%
PPA (Spot Rates)	$356.9	2.883%	11.335	-14.27%	49.69%	-8.64%
ROA = Net Interest Cost						

The PPA discount rates were 49.69% (spot rates) to 334.74% (three segment rates) higher than the Treasury STRIPS yield curve rates as of Dec. 31, 2012. This caused the liability present value (PV) calculations to be -14.27% to -38.91% lower than market valuations (Treasury STRIPS) and it shortened the modified duration by -8.64% to -23.16%. The PPA rates artificially enhanced the funded ratio by 16.6% (spot rates) to 63.7% (three segment rates), which would lower minimum contribution rates accordingly. Good job, Woody!

Pension Assets

The PPA requires that pension assets must be valued at either fair market value or a smoothed 25-year average. Furthermore, such market value must fall within a corridor of 90% to 110% of the current fair market value as of valuation date. Pre-PPA rules allowed a five-year smoothing with a corridor of 80% to 120%. Although a dramatic improvement, the option of using smoothed market values within a corridor is another way of saying that there can be a 10% margin of error. Why can't we enforce accurate and timely pension valuations so the financial truth is known to all parties affected—from the corporation plan sponsor, to the stockholders, to the pension beneficiaries—so that all affected parties can make informed financial decisions?

"You can't handle the truth."

—Jack Nicholson,
as Col. Nathan R. Jessup, in *A Few Good Men*

CHAPTER **ELEVEN**

MAP-21: FRIEND OR FOE?

On July 6, 2012, President Obama signed into law the Moving Ahead for Progress in the 21st Century Act (MAP-21). This was a highway construction bill with several amendments. It is customary for Congress to attach amendments to favorable legislation so that the odds of passing these amendments are high. Several of these amendments concerned pension topics, which were included under the following:

Part I – PENSION FUNDING STABILIZATION

Part II – PBGC PREMIUMS

Part III – IMPROVEMENTS OF PBGC

Part IV – TRANSFERS OF EXCESS PENSION ASSETS

Such legislation has been promoted as *pension relief* from higher contribution costs. On closer inspection, this legislation may very well add costs and impair the solvency of the pension plan. When the Pension Protection Act (PPA) became effective in 2008, it governed the calculation of contribution costs. A key provision concerned discount rate methodology. Beginning with the 2008 pension plan year, the discount rate methodology was changed from long Treasury rates to high quality corporate bond rates. The PPA provided plan sponsors with two discount rate options: a spot rate yield curve of current yields, or a 24-month average of a smoothed three segment yield curve (0 to five years, five to 20 years, and 20+ years). All rates were based on high quality corporate bonds (AAA and AA). Under the new MAP-21 Act, the three segment rates have been relaxed to allow corporate plan sponsors more ability to manage or manipulate the discount rates in order to reduce contribution costs.

Part I – Pension Funding Stabilization

It's almost admirable how politicians name laws in such a way as to convey solace and comfort with regard to what they have passed. Contrary to what its name implies, MAP-21 does not provide funding stabilization! It provides lower contribution costs, which actually reduces the economic funded ratio (as opposed to making a contribution which increases the funding ratio). Under MAP-21, the three segment discount rates used will be the 25-year average of each segment rate (not a 24-month average), suggesting a less volatile but much higher discount rate yield curve than the last 24-month moving average. The December 2012 25-year average discount rates under MAP-21 are higher by 228 bps (1st segment), 168 bps (2nd segment) and 124 bps (3rd segment) than the 24-month moving average. This would reduce the present value of liabilities by about 17 percent and artificially enhance the funded ratio for contribution calculations. MAP-21 also provides a corridor which allows corporations to choose discount rates between the parameters of the corridor based on whichever is the closest to the three segment rates. To determine the applicable discount rate, a corridor is established around the 25-year average three segment rates. If the 24-month average segment rate is outside the corridor, then the limit of the corridor is used. In effect, a floor and a cap are created for the current year's rate. This corridor starts at 90% to 110% in 2012, widens by 5% per year for five years, and then freezes at that level. To understand the reduction in contribution costs is to understand how the corridor reduces the present value (PV) of liabilities. The table in Exhibit 34 on the next page shows how the PV of liabilities would be reduced using both a 10-year and 15-year modified duration liability schedule based on a constant 5% three segment 24-month moving average discount rate and a constant 6.5% 25-year moving average discount rate.

EXHIBIT 34

MAP-21 DISCOUNT RATE CORRIDOR						
	Corridor		Discount Rate		PV of Liabilities Reduction	
YEAR	MIN.	MAX.	MIN.	MAX.	10-YEAR	15-YEAR
2012	90%	110%	5.85%	7.15%	-8.50%	-12.75%
2013	85%	115%	5.53%	7.48%	-5.30%	-7.95%
2014	80%	120%	5.20%	7.80%	-2.00%	-3.00%
2015	75%	125%	4.88%	8.13%	NA	NA
After 2015	70%	130%	4.55%	8.45%	NA	NA

As you can see, the minimum corridor is the closest rate to the 24-month moving average three segment rate, and will be selected until after 2014 when the rate is lower than the three segment rate and would not be selected. If we saw a trend of spiking of interest rates, the maximum corridor might be the closest to the current 24-month moving average three segment rate and be selected. The minimum corridor reduces the PV of liabilities by 8.5% to 12.75% in 2012, and to a lesser amount in 2013 and 2014. Such a hypothetical liability reduction also enhances the funded ratio and thereby reduces contribution costs. Combining the higher 25-year discount rates with a corridor adjustment could lower contribution costs significantly. The actuarial firm Mercer has estimated that such reduced contribution costs could total more than $100 billion through just 2014. Mercer has also estimated that the aggregate deficit for S&P 500 companies with a defined benefit pension plan (about 350 companies) is about -$543 billion as of June 30, 2012 (at 74% funded ratio).[52]

The government is, of course, fully aware that pension contributions are a tax deduction. As a result, reducing contribution costs should in turn raise net income, which will be taxed. Given that our corporate tax rate is now the highest in the world at 35% (averages at 39.2% including state income tax), then every $100 billion in contribution cost savings could equate to $35 billion in extra federal taxes. The federal government estimates that MAP-21 legislation will bring in **$9.394 billion in new tax revenues over 10 years**. As such, tax payments leave the company entirely, whereas contributions would become a pension asset, thereby enhancing the funded ratio and perhaps the credit rating. Another item is worth noting here. Plan sponsors need to elect which discount rate option to use. Those who selected the *spot rate curve* option now have up to one year after the date of MAP-21 enactment to switch to the new three segment option. The three segment option seems to be an unfortunate reduction in proper pension funding, which may have pension solvency implications if long term. *Caveat Emptor!*

Part II – Pensions Benefit Guaranty Corporation (PBGC) Premiums

Under Part II, PBGC premiums will be increased significantly. Single-employer premiums are raised from $35 per participant to $42 in 2013 (a 20% increase), $49 in 2014 (an additional 16.7% increase), and then indexed to inflation thereafter. Variable rate premiums for unfunded plans will rise from $9 per $1,000 on underfunding to $13 per $1000 in 2014, $18 per $1000 in 2015, and indexed to inflation

52 *US Pension Plans' Funded Status Erodes in First Half of 2012* (New York, NY: Mercer LLC, July 3, 2012). http://inside-employees-mind.mercer.com/press-releases/pension-fund-status-first-half-2012.

thereafter. Flat rate premiums for multiemployers increase from $9 to $12 per participant in 2013 and indexed to inflation thereafter. The federal government estimates this will bring in **$10.575 billion in new revenues over 10 years.**

Part III – Improvements of PBGC

PBGC had been lobbying for legislation that would give it greater control over its premium rates without any need for congressional permission. MAP-21 did not include such authority. However, it does enhance PBGC's governance. MAP-21 clarifies various requirements for board of directors' meetings and personnel by setting a five-year limit on the term of the PBGC's director, and requires a study to develop recommendations for the board and board policies. MAP-21 also establishes a plan sponsor advocate to act as a liaison between the PBGC and employee participants in terminated pension plans to ensure that such participants receive what they are entitled to under the law. The plan sponsor advocate will also help to resolve any disputes between the plan sponsor and the PBGC. Part III also requires that the PBGC contract with an outside agency to conduct an annual review of its pension insurance modeling system with internal quality review procedures.

Part IV – Transfers of Excess Pension Assets

Through Dec. 31, 2021, any plan that exceeds a 125% funded ratio may transfer these excess assets over to retiree medical benefits (OPEB) under the qualified transfer rules in Internal Revenue Code Section 420. To ascertain the funded ratio here, the MAP-21 corridors are not applicable. This option was set to expire after 2013. These transferred assets must be maintained in a separate account within the plan. Basically, only group term life insurance not in excess of $50,000 may be purchased with the transferred assets. Since

OPEB assets are not tax exempt, this transfer of assets is a taxable event. The federal government estimates this will bring in **$354 million in new tax revenues over 10 years**.

Summary

The new MAP-21 legislation, which has been labeled as "pension relief," will create **$20.323 billion in estimated federal revenues over the next 10 years as new costs for corporations**. No wonder this funding relief is scored for U.S. budget purposes as a "revenue raiser." Moreover, it reduces pension contributions which would help shore up pension funded ratios. It also penalizes unfunded pension plans with higher PBGC premiums on the unfunded amounts. Corporate plan sponsors should weigh the pros and cons of this legislation before deciding which discount rate methodology to choose. Reduced contributions today should be weighed against higher taxes, lower funded ratios, higher PBGC premiums for unfunded liabilities, potential pension solvency issues, and the loss of new pension assets. As the old adage says, "pay me now or pay me later," but you *will* pay the pension benefit some day!

"Courage is what it takes to stand up and speak. Courage is also what it takes to sit down and listen."

—Winston Churchill

CHAPTER **TWELVE**

PENSION SOLUTION: CUSTOM LIABILITY INDEX (CLI)

Most pension assets are managed versus *generic* market indexes as the index objective or benchmark. However, the true objective of a pension plan is **to fund the pension liabilities (i.e., benefit payments) at stable low contribution costs to the plan with prudent risk. No generic market index could ever represent the unique liability objective of any pension!** Just like snowflakes, no two pension plan's liabilities are alike due to each plan having a different labor force, salaries, mortality rates, and plan amendments. As pension plan sponsors have experienced too often, **given the wrong index objective: You will get the wrong risk/reward profile!**

This has been the pattern for most pension plans as their funded ratios have been on a roller coaster for several decades. Until the true liability objective (and any liability driven objective) of a pension plan is measured frequently and accurately, pension assets are in jeopardy of being managed to the wrong index objective. Until a **custom liability index** is built and installed as the proper benchmark, all asset decisions are in danger of being mismanaged and misaligned with the true liability objective. Asset allocation, asset management and performance measurement are all index driven. Until assets and liabilities are "marked to market" accurately and frequently, the funded ratio is in jeopardy of being calculated incorrectly and too delinquently to be of any value. Given the wrong funded ratio, asset allocation will function inappropriately. It follows that a pension plan with a surplus should have a different asset allocation than a plan with a large deficit. Such funded ratios need to be based on market or *economic* valuations, not accounting or actuarial valuations. Given the wrong index objective, asset management will behave accordingly and produce an inappropriate risk/reward profile (similar to the index benchmark). Similarly, given the wrong index objective, performance measurement will then provide inappropriate risk/reward measurements. It is rare that pension assets are ever compared to pension liabilities in performance measurement reports. It follows that if you **outperform the S&P 500 (or any market index) but lose to liability growth, the pension plan loses!** All asset-related functions and decisions should be based on the liability objective. This misalignment of assets versus the true liability objective has created a funded ratio roller coaster which led to a significant escalation of contribution costs, earnings drag, and credit ratings deterioration... it all links. Using a static asset allocation of 5% Cash (Ryan three-month T-Bill Index), 30% Bonds (Lehman/Barclays Aggregate), 60% Equity (S&P 500) and 5% Int'l (EAFE) versus the Ryan Liability Benchmark Index (equal weighting of Treasury STRIPS from 1 year to 30 years) we get a good picture of the funded ratio roller coaster starting at 100.00 as of Dec. 31, 1988 (see Exhibit 35, next page).

The Pension Scoreboard

Just like the scoreboard at a ball game, the pension scoreboard dictates your pension strategy. The behavior of a team that's way behind will be very different from that of a team that's way ahead. The Pension Protection Act and current accounting rules act as an annual

EXHIBIT 35

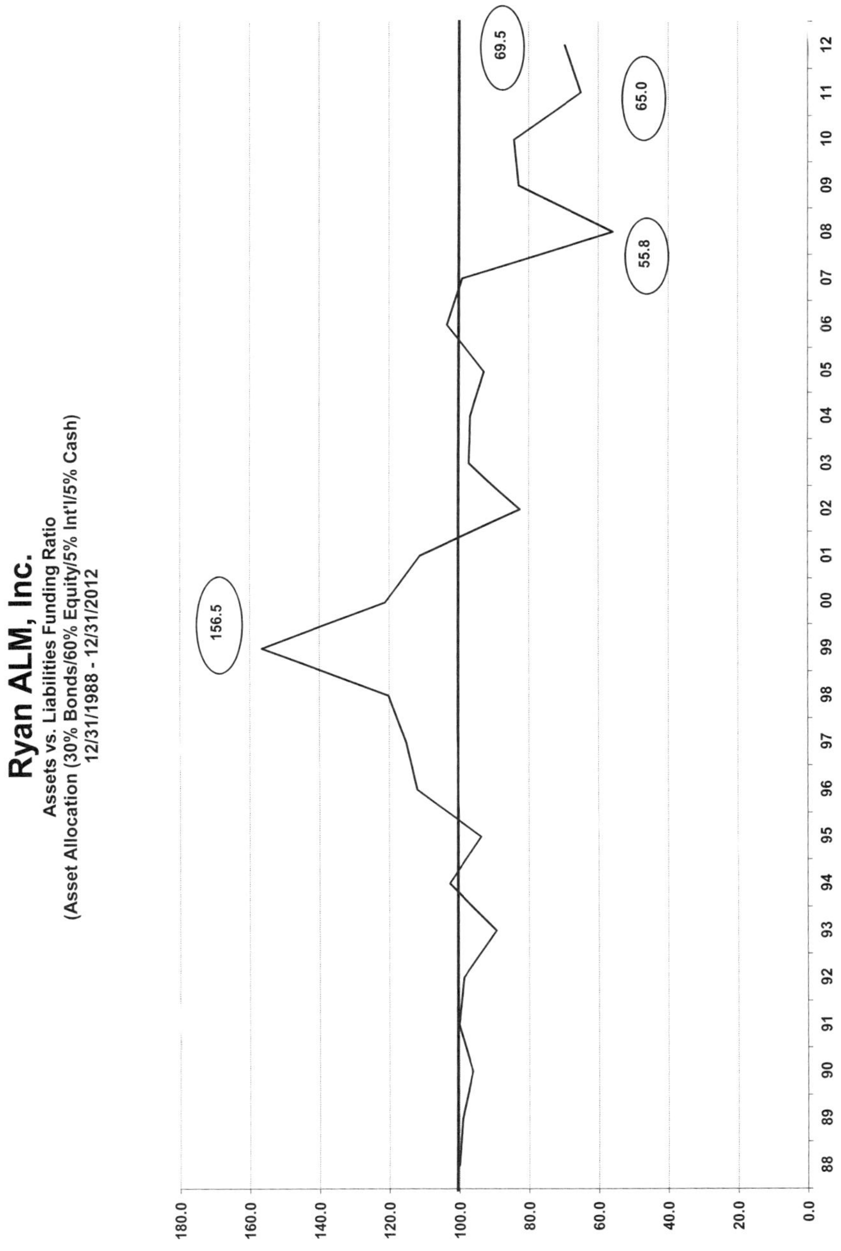

Ryan ALM, Inc.
Assets vs. Liabilities Funding Ratio
(Asset Allocation (30% Bonds/60% Equity/5% Int'l/5% Cash)
12/31/1988 - 12/31/2012
156.5
55.8
65.0
69.5

scoreboard, requiring the posting of each team's score (asset team vs. liability team) at the end of the fiscal year. This score will decide the pension contribution (if any) that is needed for the next year, the pension expense or income, and the funded ratio, all of which affect earnings and the credit rating. Accordingly, it is critical that a pension scoreboard correctly and frequently displays the score in terms of year-to-date growth rate and the size of pension assets versus pension liabilities, thereby correctly calculating the economic funded ratio and resulting surplus or deficit. To accomplish this objective accurately requires the construction of a liability index customized to the specific pension plan's liability schedule and broken out by term structure (i.e., a yield curve). A custom liability index allows the pension board of trustees and the pension consultant to ascertain the true economic funded ratio, as well as the true relative growth of assets versus liabilities (i.e., total plan performance measurement) at every board meeting. This information is critical in helping the board decide on asset allocation, benefit, and contribution decisions. Moreover, a custom liability index broken out by term structure provides proper data so asset management can function effectively such that short assets can understand and monitor their funding opponent: short liabilities; intermediate assets can understand and monitor their funding opponent: intermediate liabilities; and long assets can understand and monitor their funding opponent: long liabilities. Without a custom liability index, several fundamental dilemmas can develop:

Traditional Bond Indexes

As the former director of research at Lehman Brothers, (now Barclays Capital), I designed the Lehman Government/Corporate, Lehman Aggregate, and about 60 other popular Lehman bond indexes. In the late 1970s, I approached the consultant industry to gain acceptance for our indexes as the appropriate benchmarks for fixed income. I think I did too good of a job. In a short period of time, the Lehman indexes were the bond benchmarks throughout America. Many asset managers have been hired and fired based on their relative performance to these Lehman bond indexes, especially the Lehman (now Barclays) Aggregate.

Several pension plans have accepted generic bond market indexes as a proxy for liabilities. Traditional generic bond indexes do a good job of measuring the risk/reward behavior of a bond market sector or universe, but have nothing to do with pension liabilities. It is mission impossible for any generic index to measure the unique cash flows of any pension, much less be the benchmark for a universe of pension plans. How could one generic index ever represent the vast array of liability schedules and cash flows? Only a custom liability index could ever measure and monitor the risk/reward behavior of any pension liability cash flow schedule. As proof of this reality, let's examine the amazing risk/reward track record of the Lehman/Barclays Aggregate index versus Treasury STRIPS yield curve indexes. In 1985, when STRIPS were born, I designed the Ryan STRIPS Indexes as a series of constant maturity/duration indexes from 1-year to 30-years (30 separate indexes). These Ryan STRIPS Indexes are a good proxy for the risk/reward behavior of liabilities. It is hard to believe that the Lehman/Barclays Aggregate index, which is heavily skewed to non-Treasuries, would underperform Treasury STRIPS over long horizons. However, as shown in Exhibit 36, when comparing the Lehman/Barclays Aggregate index to the Ryan Liability Benchmark Index (equal weighting of the Ryan STRIPS Indexes) as the liability proxy, the Lehman/Barclays Aggregate index has severely underperformed liability growth rates for the last 26 years by -2.49% annually since 1986!

EXHIBIT 36

Ryan ALM, Inc.
Performance Attribution Report (PAR)

Horizon : 12/31/1986 to 12/31/2012		Barclays AGG	Ryan Liability (Benchmark)	Difference
RISK				
1. Annualized Standard Deviation	%	3.92	13.02	-9.10
2. Volatility to Benchmark (Beta)		0.26		
3. R-Square	%	75.90		
4. Correlation	%	87.12		
5. STD of Differential Return	bp	283		
6. Tracking Deviation	bp	214		
7. Shortfall Frequency	%	53.21		
8. Average Shortfall	bp	224		
REWARD				
9. Annualized Total Return	%	7.06	9.46	-2.40
10. Cumulative Total Return	%	489.78	949.74	-459.96
11. Excess Return Frequency	%	46.79		
12. Average Excess Return	bp	202		
RISK ADJUSTED RETURNS				
13. Sharpe's Ratio (old)		0.76	0.41	0.34
14. Information Ratio		-0.24		

All calculations are based on monthly returns.

Moreover, the Lehman/Barclays Aggregate index has a very poor correlation history versus liabilities. This risk/reward disparity between the Lehman/Barclays Aggregate index and the Ryan Liability Benchmark Index actually increased from Dec. 31, 1999, through Dec. 31, 2012, with the annualized standard deviation (STD) increasing from -9.10% to -9.95%, and the annualized total return difference widening from -2.40% to -3.80% (see Exhibit 37 on the next page).

As mentioned earlier, on the day in early 1985 when the government created the Treasury STRIPS, my index team at Ryan Financial Strategy Group built the first Treasury STRIPS yield curve indexes. This led us to produce the **Ryan Liability Benchmark Index and the Ryan ALM Custom Liability Index as the proper benchmark concept for liability driven objectives.** The logic was that no generic index could replicate the unique cash flows of any pension or liability objective (e.g., those of insurance, lotteries, OPEB, etc.). Since interest rate risk, or systematic risk, dominates any bond or liability portfolio, it was critical that the liability benchmark represents the interest rate sensitivity of the liability objective. Most pensions have long average durations of 10 to 15 years (OPEB liabilities, at 15 to 25 years, are even longer). The Lehman/Barclays Aggregate index and the Lehman/Barclays Government/Corporate index tend to have average durations of around five years. One would think that these index features were obvious facts that would cause dismissal of generic bond indexes such as the Lehman/Barclays Aggregate index as the proper benchmark for liability driven objectives. The risk/reward mismatch of the Lehman/Barclays Aggregate index versus any liability objective is potentially significant and costly (especially in contribution costs and opportunity costs).

Over time, many pension plan sponsors and their consultants have recognized this interest rate risk behavior disparity, and are replacing their traditional fixed income benchmark (i.e., Lehman/

EXHIBIT 37

Ryan ALM, Inc.
Performance Attribution Report (PAR)

Horizon : 12/31/1999 to 12/31/2012		Barclays AGG	Ryan Liability (Benchmark)	Difference
RISK				
1. Annualized Standard Deviation	%	3.54	13.48	-9.95
2. Volatility to Benchmark (Beta)		0.21		
3. R-Square	%	66.69		
4. Correlation	%	81.66		
5. STD of Differential Return	bp	312		
6. Tracking Deviation	bp	233		
7. Shortfall Frequency	%	57.05		
8. Average Shortfall	bp	236		
REWARD				
9. Annualized Total Return	%	6.30	10.10	-3.80
10. Cumulative Total Return	%	121.30	249.50	-128.21
11. Excess Return Frequency	%	42.95		
12. Average Excess Return	bp	228		
RISK ADJUSTED RETURNS				
13. Sharpe's Ratio (old)		1.10	0.57	0.53
14. Information Ratio		-0.35		

All calculations are based on monthly returns.

Barclays Aggregate index) with a longer duration index (i.e., long Lehman/Barclays Government/Corporate index). Although a longer duration, the long Lehman/Barclays Government/Corporate index and in fact any generic bond index, have structural flaws that should disqualify them as a liability benchmark. Examples include:

Coupon Bonds vs. Zero Coupon Bonds

Generic bond indexes only use coupon bonds as the portfolio composition. **It is mathematically impossible for coupon bonds to have durations longer than 19 years!** As a result, they could never price or match any liabilities greater than 19 years. For most pensions, this represents 30% to 50% of their liabilities. OPEB liabilities would be even higher. Coupon bonds also have reinvestment risk, which creates uncertain cash flows and uncertain future values. For this reason, liability matching strategies (i.e., defeasance, dedication, immunization) tend not to favor coupon bonds. Moreover, one generic index has one cash flow schedule. How could one generic index's cash flow schedule fit so many pensions? How could so many pensions fit into the same shoe?

Market Weighted vs. Liability Weighted

The most popular generic bond market indexes are all *market weighted*. In order to market weight a bond index you must know the amount outstanding. As simple as it sounds, it is most difficult, if not impossible, to know the amount outstanding on bonds. Treasury bonds are *stripped* and reported delinquently. Agency bonds are *stripped* and not reported at all. This is why generic bond indexes leave the original issue amount on Government issues as the amount outstanding. Imagine a $10 billion Treasury bond that is 40% stripped, leaving a $6 billion float available to trade but showing $10 billion outstanding for its market weight calculation (i.e., 40% weighting error). Corporate bonds are tendered, sunk, and put, which is usually only reported annually in the 10-K financial report. Mortgage-backed securities have monthly principal payments and prepayments that are reported weeks delinquently. As a result, it is "mission impossible" for any generic bond index to know and report the accurate amount outstanding for most bonds at the end of the month for rebalancing and return calculation purposes. The obvious conclusion is that ***market-weighted* bond indexes are *skewed* and faulty data.**

The most appropriate weighting for liability driven objectives is *liability weighted*, based upon the clients' actuarial liability projections so that an accurate duration, present value, term structure, growth rate, and interest rate sensitivity can be calculated. Only a custom liability index weighted by the client's actuarial projections is in harmony with the true client objective. Existing corporate bonds and mortgage-backed securities do not qualify as liability discount rates due to their lack of zero coupons, uncertain cash flows, shorter durations, and credit risk.

In the sample Ryan ALM Custom Liability Index (CLI) shown in Exhibit 38 on the following page, a linear $20 million per year benefit payment schedule is used. This is then divided by 12 to determine a monthly liability payment schedule. Each monthly liability payment is then priced off the Treasury STRIPS yield curve as a discount rate series or yield curve. The CLI is providing an accurate economic valuation such that any pension plan sponsor could actually buy the CLI as a liability index fund to settle or defease the liabilities. The CLI produces a daily structure report calculating critical statistical data.

A common mistake is made by matching the *average* duration of liabilities instead of matching the entire term structure of liabilities.

EXHIBIT 38

Ryan ALM Custom Liability Index
TSY STRIP - Structure
12/31/2012

Duration Cells	% Weight	# Payments	Future Value	Present Value	Averages Coupon	Price	YTW	MDUR
SHORT(0-1)	4.80	2	20,000,000	19,970,805	0.00	99.854	0.186	0.747
01.01 - 02.50	7.16	3	30,000,000	29,814,805	0.00	99.383	0.303	1.990
02.50 - 03.50	4.73	2	20,000,000	19,703,836	0.00	98.520	0.457	3.233
03.50 - 04.50	4.67	2	20,000,000	19,452,490	0.00	97.264	0.653	4.220
04.50 - 05.50	4.59	2	20,000,000	19,122,518	0.00	95.615	0.856	5.202
05.50 - 06.50	4.49	2	20,000,000	18,705,499	0.00	93.531	1.074	6.180
06.50 - 07.50	4.37	2	20,000,000	18,194,721	0.00	90.978	1.312	7.152
07.50 - 08.50	4.23	2	20,000,000	17,609,572	0.00	88.054	1.553	8.119
08.50 - 09.50	4.08	2	20,000,000	17,001,976	0.00	85.017	1.770	9.085
09.50 - 10.50	3.93	2	20,000,000	16,362,657	0.00	81.821	1.977	10.047
INTER(1- 10.50)	42.27	19	190,000,000	175,968,073	0.00	92.997	1.028	5.752
10.50 - 11.50	3.78	2	20,000,000	15,736,053	0.00	78.688	2.154	11.008
11.50 - 12.50	3.63	2	20,000,000	15,111,961	0.00	75.567	2.314	11.968
12.50 - 13.50	3.48	2	20,000,000	14,507,594	0.00	72.546	2.452	12.928
13.50 - 14.50	3.34	2	20,000,000	13,919,410	0.00	69.604	2.576	13.888
14.50 - 15.50	3.22	2	20,000,000	13,388,892	0.00	66.950	2.667	14.850
15.50 - 16.50	3.10	2	20,000,000	12,890,496	0.00	64.457	2.740	15.813
16.50 - 17.50	2.99	2	20,000,000	12,442,421	0.00	62.218	2.790	16.777
17.50 - 18.50	2.88	2	20,000,000	11,993,523	0.00	59.973	2.842	17.742
18.50 - 19.50	2.78	2	20,000,000	11,556,959	0.00	57.790	2.890	18.705
19.50 - 20.50	2.68	2	20,000,000	11,141,324	0.00	55.711	2.932	19.669
LONG(10.5 - 20.5)	31.87	20	200,000,000	132,688,633	0.00	67.156	2.609	15.031
20.50 - 21.51	2.58	2	20,000,000	10,738,156	0.00	53.696	2.970	20.633
21.50 - 22.50	2.48	2	20,000,000	10,344,171	0.00	51.725	3.008	21.596
22.50 - 23.50	2.40	2	20,000,000	10,009,291	0.00	50.051	3.022	22.564
23.50 - 24.50	2.31	2	20,000,000	9,628,506	0.00	48.147	3.061	23.526
24.50 - 25.50	2.23	2	20,000,000	9,271,996	0.00	46.364	3.092	24.489
25.50 - 26.50	2.14	2	20,000,000	8,919,792	0.00	44.603	3.124	25.450
26.50 - 27.50	2.07	2	20,000,000	8,596,877	0.00	42.987	3.147	26.415
27.50 - 28.50	1.99	2	20,000,000	8,291,869	0.00	41.463	3.166	27.379
28.50 - 29.50	1.92	2	20,000,000	7,981,363	0.00	39.909	3.191	28.342
29.50 - 30.50	0.94	1	10,000,000	3,897,402	0.00	38.974	3.191	29.072
VLONG(20.5+)	21.06	19	190,000,000	87,679,422	0.00	46.621	3.085	24.464
Total	100.00	60	600,000,000	416,306,932	0.00	75.322	1.925	12.410

The projected liability payment schedule is a *yield curve* of cash flows. You must match *every* liability payment to be considered matched, not just the average duration. This is the problem with immunization strategies. In the CLI shown in Exhibit 37, the average modified duration is 12.573 years. You could not purchase one Treasury STRIPS with that modified duration to match or fund the entire liability term structure. As soon as the yield curve changes its shape (this takes about an hour on most Treasury trading days), you are no longer matched. Further, how could you *fund* a liability term structure with one long duration bond? You would have great market risk that the one bond would not match or behave similarly to the risk/reward of each liability payment it is funding. This would be most evident in a secular trend to higher rates as the one long duration bond would suffer negative price return and lose value when each liability payment became due. The classic example of this asset/liability matching confusion is the 30-year Treasury coupon bond, which is stripped and reconstituted on a regular (if not daily) basis. Although in future value, the pieces equal the whole, there is an arbitrage in present values where the pieces do *not* equal the whole. This is the major trading reason for stripping and reconstitution. **In order to match liabilities, you have to match the entire term structure (i.e., all liability payments), not just the average duration.**

Interest Rate Risk Sensitivity

An eight-year study published in 1992 by Notre Dame Profs. Frank Reilly, Ph.D., David Wright, Ph.D., and Wenchi Kao, Ph.D., proved that interest rate risk accounted for over 98% of the risk in bonds using all of the popular investment grade bond indexes of that time.[53] With such a critical cause of the risk/reward behavior in bonds, you would think that bond indexes would provide interest rate sensitiv-

53 Frank K. Reilly, G. Wenchi Kao, and David J. Wright, "Alternative Bond Market Indexes," Financial Analysts Journal 48, no. 3 (May/June 1992). http://www.ryanalm.com/portals/5/research/Notre-Dame-Study-of-Bond-Indexes.pdf.

ity tests as part of their reporting process. Yet such reports are rare, leaving it up to the investor to understand and test for such dominant systematic risk. Notably, insurance companies are mandated by their NAIC rules to produce an annual test of their interest rate sensitivity on assets versus liabilities to understand the solvency effect. (This test usually shocks assets and liabilities by 300 basis points.) You would think that the pension industry would mandate similar interest rate sensitivity rules. If you use government zero-coupon bonds to price pension liabilities, interest rate risk is close to 100% of the risk/reward behavior. To monitor such behavior, the Ryan ALM Custom Liability Index (CLI) was designed to include two interest rate sensitivity reports, providing:

1. Growth rate of liabilities, given four interest rate movements

2. Ending present values, given the same four interest rate movements

As you can see in Exhibits 39 and 40, the CLI is quite interest rate sensitive. With just a 100-basis-points discount rate change in either direction, liability growth is quite volatile (moving from **-9.34% to +15.85% total return**) with just a 12.573-year duration.

EXHIBIT 39

Ryan ALM Custom Liability Index
TSY STRIP Sensitivity - Total Return Based on Interest Rate Moves over 12-Month Horizon
12/31/2012

Duration Cells	% Weight	Future Value	Present Value	YTW	MDur	100	50	-50	-100
SHORT(0-1)	4.80	20,000,000	19,970,805	0.186	0.747				
01.01 - 02.50	7.16	30,000,000	29,814,805	0.303	1.990	-0.68	-0.19	0.80	1.31
02.50 - 03.50	4.73	20,000,000	19,703,836	0.457	3.233	-1.75	-0.66	1.59	2.74
03.50 - 04.50	4.67	20,000,000	19,452,490	0.653	4.220	-2.53	-0.95	2.29	3.97
04.50 - 05.50	4.59	20,000,000	19,122,518	0.856	5.202	-3.28	-1.24	3.01	5.22
05.50 - 06.50	4.49	20,000,000	18,705,499	1.074	6.180	-4.01	-1.51	3.74	6.49
06.50 - 07.50	4.37	20,000,000	18,194,721	1.312	7.152	-4.72	-1.76	4.49	7.79
07.50 - 08.50	4.23	20,000,000	17,609,572	1.553	8.119	-5.41	-2.00	5.25	9.10
08.50 - 09.50	4.08	20,000,000	17,001,976	1.770	9.085	-6.11	-2.26	5.99	10.40
09.50 - 10.50	3.93	20,000,000	16,362,657	1.977	10.047	-6.82	-2.53	6.72	11.70
INTER(1- 10.50)	42.27	190,000,000	175,968,073	1.028	5.752	-3.63	-1.34	3.49	6.03
10.50 - 11.50	3.78	20,000,000	15,736,053	2.154	11.008	-7.55	-2.83	7.42	12.99
11.50 - 12.50	3.63	20,000,000	15,111,961	2.314	11.968	-8.29	-3.14	8.11	14.26
12.50 - 13.50	3.48	20,000,000	14,507,594	2.452	12.928	-9.04	-3.48	8.78	15.53
13.50 - 14.50	3.34	20,000,000	13,919,410	2.576	13.888	-9.79	-3.82	9.43	16.79
14.50 - 15.50	3.22	20,000,000	13,388,892	2.667	14.850	-10.57	-4.20	10.06	18.03
15.50 - 16.50	3.10	20,000,000	12,890,496	2.740	15.813	-11.36	-4.59	10.67	19.26
16.50 - 17.50	2.99	20,000,000	12,442,421	2.790	16.777	-12.17	-5.00	11.26	20.48
17.50 - 18.50	2.88	20,000,000	11,993,523	2.842	17.742	-12.96	-5.41	11.86	21.72
18.50 - 19.50	2.78	20,000,000	11,556,959	2.890	18.705	-13.76	-5.82	12.45	22.96
19.50 - 20.50	2.68	20,000,000	11,141,324	2.932	19.669	-14.54	-6.23	13.04	24.21
LONG(10.5 - 20.5)	31.87	200,000,000	132,688,633	2.609	15.031	-10.76	-4.33	10.11	18.23
20.50 - 21.51	2.58	20,000,000	10,738,156	2.970	20.633	-15.33	-6.65	13.63	25.46
21.50 - 22.50	2.48	20,000,000	10,344,171	3.008	21.596	-16.11	-7.06	14.23	26.73
22.50 - 23.50	2.40	20,000,000	10,009,291	3.022	22.564	-16.90	-7.50	14.80	27.99
23.50 - 24.50	2.31	20,000,000	9,628,506	3.061	23.526	-17.66	-7.91	15.40	29.28
24.50 - 25.50	2.23	20,000,000	9,271,996	3.092	24.489	-18.42	-8.32	15.99	30.58
25.50 - 26.50	2.14	20,000,000	8,919,792	3.124	25.450	-19.17	-8.73	16.59	31.89
26.50 - 27.50	2.07	20,000,000	8,596,877	3.147	26.415	-19.93	-9.15	17.18	33.20
27.50 - 28.50	1.99	20,000,000	8,291,869	3.166	27.379	-20.68	-9.57	17.77	34.52
28.50 - 29.50	1.92	20,000,000	7,981,363	3.191	28.342	-21.42	-9.98	18.37	35.86
29.50 - 30.50	0.94	10,000,000	3,897,402	3.191	29.072	-21.99	-10.31	18.80	36.86
VLONG(20.5+)	21.06	190,000,000	87,679,422	3.085	24.464	-18.38	-8.31	15.98	30.58
Total	100.00	600,000,000	416,306,932	1.925	12.410	-9.28	-3.88	8.47	15.55

EXHIBIT 40

Ryan ALM Custom Liability Index

TSY STRIP Sensitivity - Market Value Based on Interest Rate Moves over 12-Month Horizon

12/31/2012

Duration Cells	% Weight	Future Value	Present Value	YTW	MDur	100	50	-50	-100
SHORT(0-1)	4.80	20,000,000	19,970,805	0.186	0.747				
01.01 - 02.50	7.16	30,000,000	29,814,805	0.303	1.990	29,610,896	29,757,188	30,054,345	30,205,258
02.50 - 03.50	4.73	20,000,000	19,703,836	0.457	3.233	19,358,254	19,574,337	20,017,176	20,244,087
03.50 - 04.50	4.67	20,000,000	19,452,490	0.653	4.220	18,960,977	19,266,954	19,898,640	20,224,700
04.50 - 05.50	4.59	20,000,000	19,122,518	0.856	5.202	18,494,887	18,885,420	19,697,614	20,119,933
05.50 - 06.50	4.49	20,000,000	18,705,499	1.074	6.180	17,954,766	18,423,285	19,404,828	19,918,944
06.50 - 07.50	4.37	20,000,000	18,194,721	1.312	7.152	17,336,550	17,875,209	19,011,957	19,611,707
07.50 - 08.50	4.23	20,000,000	17,609,572	1.553	8.119	16,657,489	17,257,921	18,534,273	19,212,559
08.50 - 09.50	4.08	20,000,000	17,001,976	1.770	9.085	15,962,667	16,617,658	18,020,134	18,770,834
09.50 - 10.50	3.93	20,000,000	16,362,657	1.977	10.047	15,246,642	15,948,392	17,461,914	18,277,888
INTER(1- 10.50)	42.27	190,000,000	175,968,073	1.028	5.752	169,583,128	173,606,365	182,100,882	186,585,911
10.50 - 11.50	3.78	20,000,000	15,736,053	2.154	11.008	14,548,080	15,290,612	16,903,741	17,779,671
11.50 - 12.50	3.63	20,000,000	15,111,961	2.314	11.968	13,859,708	14,636,817	16,337,336	17,267,346
12.50 - 13.50	3.48	20,000,000	14,507,594	2.452	12.928	13,196,630	14,003,203	15,781,034	16,760,296
13.50 - 14.50	3.34	20,000,000	13,919,410	2.576	13.888	12,556,260	13,387,386	15,232,667	16,256,362
14.50 - 15.50	3.22	20,000,000	13,388,892	2.667	14.850	11,973,071	12,826,757	14,735,971	15,802,733
15.50 - 16.50	3.10	20,000,000	12,890,496	2.740	15.813	11,425,545	12,298,880	14,266,325	15,373,512
16.50 - 17.50	2.99	20,000,000	12,442,421	2.790	16.777	10,928,220	11,820,049	13,843,896	14,991,008
17.50 - 18.50	2.88	20,000,000	11,993,523	2.842	17.742	10,438,607	11,344,667	13,415,897	14,598,288
18.50 - 19.50	2.78	20,000,000	11,556,959	2.890	18.705	9,967,296	10,884,406	12,996,282	14,210,513
19.50 - 20.50	2.68	20,000,000	11,141,324	2.932	19.669	9,520,874	10,446,802	12,594,650	13,838,410
LONG(10.5 - 20.5)	31.87	200,000,000	132,688,633	2.609	15.031	118,414,291	126,939,578	146,107,800	156,878,137
20.50 - 21.51	2.58	20,000,000	10,738,156	2.970	20.633	9,092,128	10,024,219	12,202,262	13,472,531
21.50 - 22.50	2.48	20,000,000	10,344,171	3.008	21.596	8,678,095	9,613,626	11,815,790	13,109,306
22.50 - 23.50	2.40	20,000,000	10,009,291	3.022	22.564	8,317,854	9,258,912	11,490,462	12,810,637
23.50 - 24.50	2.31	20,000,000	9,628,506	3.061	23.526	7,928,102	8,867,321	11,110,893	12,447,637
24.50 - 25.50	2.23	20,000,000	9,271,996	3.092	24.489	7,563,974	8,500,614	10,754,522	12,106,996
25.50 - 26.50	2.14	20,000,000	8,919,792	3.124	25.450	7,209,577	8,141,125	10,399,295	11,763,964
26.50 - 27.50	2.07	20,000,000	8,596,877	3.147	26.415	6,883,757	7,810,505	10,073,641	11,451,054
27.50 - 28.50	1.99	20,000,000	8,291,869	3.166	27.379	6,577,298	7,498,604	9,765,094	11,154,369
28.50 - 29.50	1.92	20,000,000	7,981,363	3.191	28.342	6,272,109	7,184,934	9,447,165	10,843,678
29.50 - 30.50	0.94	10,000,000	3,897,402	3.191	29.072	3,040,553	3,495,730	4,630,094	5,334,114
VLONG(20.5+)	21.06	190,000,000	87,679,422	3.085	24.464	71,563,446	80,395,590	101,689,217	114,494,286
Total	100.00	600,000,000	416,306,932	1.925	12.410	359,560,865	380,941,533	429,897,898	457,958,334

Also noteworthy is that the performance (total return) or growth rate of liabilities is not symmetrical. This is because income return is always a positive return, as shown in Exhibit 41.

EXHIBIT 41

INTEREST RATE SENSITIVITY OF CUSTOM LIABILITY INDEX				
	Growth Rate		Ending Present Value	
Present Value	+ 100bps	-100 bps	+100 bps	-100 bps
$416,306,932	-9.28%	15.55%	$359,560,865	$457,958,334

Funded Ratio

The true economic funded ratio should be the focus of asset allocation, benefit, and contribution decisions. A large deficit should have a different asset allocation than a small deficit or surplus position. ***It is critical that the liability index benchmark measures and prices the liabilities of the pension plan—not the bond market!*** To reiterate and reemphasize, just like snowflakes, you will never find two liability schedules that are exactly alike. This is a serious consideration when choosing a benchmark for liabilities and why only a custom liability index fits. Given accurate and frequent liability valuation information, the pension plan trustees and consultants are now in a much more informed position to execute their duties. Generic bond indexes tell you nothing about the plan liabilities and could very well misinform and misdirect any asset allocation, benefit, or contribution decision. A liability driven objective needs a ***custom liability index***, not a generic bond index!

UBS/iBoxx Liability Indexes

On Oct. 18, 2006, UBS announced that it had partnered with International Index Company (IIC) to launch a suite of iBoxx US Pension Liability Indices. Namely, a three-index set of benchmarks that seeks to mimic pension liability performance:

1. **Aggregate Index** – Designed to mimic the overall performance of a representative defined benefit plan in the US.

2. **Active Index** – Designed to mimic the overall performance of an active (non-retired) member liability profile.

3. **Retired Index** – Designed to mimic the overall performance of a retired member liability profile for a model US defined benefit plan.

UBS correctly points out that developing an investment policy for a pension plan necessitates managing and stabilizing the volatility of the funded ratio. Investment strategies that consider or manage the funded ratio, such that asset growth equals or exceeds liability growth, are required.

It is good that UBS acknowledges that a pension has retired life and active life components that behave differently. It is also good that UBS acknowledges and uses the words *performance of liability* to suggest a volatile growth or total return behavior, such that the total returns of assets should be compared to the total return of liabilities. It is great that UBS also acknowledges that **a pension fund investment policy and strategy should be to manage the volatility of their funding ratio**—right on! What is wrong here is the use of generic indices to capture the liability growth behavior of each and every pension plan situation. Similar to Cinderella's slippers, no generic index could possibly price or value every, or even several, pension fund benefit payment schedules. **The truth is that each**

pension fund is unique; each has a different labor force, different mortality, different salary structure, and certainly different plan amendments. The differences can be enormous, resulting in a wide array of durations, term structures, and interest rate sensitivity. The error in calculating or portraying the risk/reward behavior of each clients' liabilities using generic indexes rather than custom liability indexes can be quite significant and critical. Using generic indexes would result in erroneous liability growth rates and funded ratios, which in turn would affect investment asset allocation decisions.

Longevity Indexes

In early 2006, Credit Suisse introduced its Longevity Index as a standardized measure of the expected average lifetime for a general population. Its 2006 U.S. Composite Index value was 80.6 years. **There are no securities in this index!** Once again, a generic index could never fit the unique and varied term structures of a pension cash flow schedule. There have been very few longevity bonds ever issued. The Swiss Re Mortality bond was issued in December 2003 with a maturity of January 2007 for $400 million. The other bond of note was a BNP Paribas Longevity bond that was announced November 2004 with a 25-year maturity, but withdrawn due to lack of interest. Credit Suisse believes its new index will promote the use of longevity swaps and longevity-structured notes. Longevity indexes might be an interesting study or tool, but certainly are not a proper benchmark for liabilities for all the reasons repeated throughout this book: The index doesn't match or defease liabilities, it is not a yield curve, one cannot buy it, and it is certainly not customized to each client's unique cash flow schedule.

Lehman/Barclays Liability Indexes

Lehman introduced its Zero Coupon Nominal Swaps and Zero Coupon Inflation Swaps indices. Lehman's research report as of December 2006 made it clear that the popular Lehman Aggregate, Long Government/Credit indices are not a good fit as benchmarks for pensions and any LDI objective—*Alleluia!* Lehman also questions or cautions on the use of these new indexes as liability benchmarks with the statement, "These techniques, which provide the advantage of simplicity, nevertheless present a number of limitations. While the duration of the benchmark may closely resemble that of the liability stream, the term structure differential between the benchmark and liabilities could be significant, leaving exposure to changes in the shape of the curve. For liability streams that are frozen, an added challenge is presented by the index turnover each month that will hold the duration somewhat constant, while the liabilities will decrease in duration over time, causing an undesired duration drift between the two."[54] Well said by Lehman. They should be congratulated for their integrity and foresight here. No generic index could ever match or represent the unique cash flow of a pension benefit payment schedule. Only a custom liability index is the approximate liability benchmark for pension assets to manage and be measured against, as well as the most accurate way to price and value liabilities (i.e., discount rates).

Society of Actuaries (SOA) Research

In October 2004, the Society of Actuaries (SOA) Task Force on Asset Liability Management Principles released an exposure draft "Principles Underlying Asset Liability Management." In the exposure draft they state succinctly the need to value liabilities at the market (i.e., economic books):

A consistent ALM structure can only be achieved for econom-

54 Lehman Bros. Fixed Income Research "Global Family of Indexes" page 88, December 2006.

> ic objectives...[Accounting] measures can sometimes distort economic reality and produce results inconsistent with economic value. Because ALM is concerned with the future asset and liability cash flows, the natural focus of ALM is economic value...Entities that focus on economic value tend to achieve their financial objectives more consistently in the long term.

Translation: Pension plans need to create a set of economic books so asset/liability management (ALM) can function effectively.

Ryan ALM Custom Liability Indexes

In 1985 when STRIPS were born, my index team at Ryan Financial Services Group and I designed the first **Treasury STRIPS Index** series. In 1991, we weighted those indexes to any client's unique liability cash flow schedule to create the first **custom liability index**. We developed a generic version with static equal weights for educational purposes, and a weighted version that best represents each client's actuarially defined cash flow schedule as the proper liability benchmark. Since 1991, my team and I have created hundreds of custom liability indexes for every type of liability driven client (e.g., pensions, lotteries, NDT, healthcare, and insurance).

I believe that a custom liability index composed of Treasury STRIPS best fits the true client objective and best complies with the SOA research, FAS No. 87, FAS No. 106, and now FAS No. 158 (ASC 715). In addition to pricing liabilities at the market (STRIPS), Ryan ALM provides all discount rates in conformity to ASC 715 (formally FAS 158), PPA (both three segment and spot rates), and GASB (fixed single rate). The SOA states that until a set of ***economic books*** are created that monitor the market value of liabilities, assets cannot be managed effectively for a liability driven objective. FASB repeats and stresses that the discount rates to be used should be a ***zero-coupon portfolio*** as the ***settlement rate(s)*** since only a zero-coupon bond has a certain future value. This means a rate that can settle or defease the liability. It must be a rate that can be purchased, not a hypothetical rate. There must be a rate for each monthly benefit payment. Any index or discount rate methodology that cannot settle liabilities and cannot be customized to the unique cash flow term structure of every client should not be used as a benchmark for asset management purposes for a liability driven objective (ALM). Each client's liability schedule is unique to them. They each have a different labor force, different salaries, different mortality, different plan amendments, and different benefits. How could any generic index represent and price such a unique set of data? Moreover, how could we use a single discount rate as *the* discount rate as public plans feel required to do in conformity to GASB accounting? Liabilities are a term structure, or yield curve, of monthly benefit payments. Each payment has to be priced and valued distinctly and separately. If you cannot defease each liability payment with the discount rate methodology, then such rates are economically unfit. The FAS No. 158 and FAS No. 106 rules make it clear that only a zero-coupon bond portfolio of high quality bonds should be used as the discount rates. In the bond market today, only Treasury zero-coupon bonds exist as a yield curve of high-quality zero-coupon securities that have sizable liquidity. Manufactured high-quality corporate zero-coupon securities also qualify as discount rates under ASC 715.

Pension Solution: Custom Liability Index (CLI)

Only a custom liability index (CLI) could ever price and match the unique cash flows of any pension or liability driven objective. It is critical that the CLI is installed as the proper benchmark for assets. Once in place, the asset side can now function effectively with regard to asset allocation, asset management, and performance measurement in harmony with the true client objective. With a CLI, the economic funded ratio (or market value of assets/liabilities) can now be calculated accurately and frequently, whereas traditionally it was reviewed only once a year (months after the end of the fiscal year) using accounting or actuarial valuations. Once the economic funded ratio has been calculated, the board of trustees can make well-informed asset allocation, benefit, and contribution decisions...it all links! **The funded ratio should be the focus of asset allocation,** such that a large deficit position has a radically different allocation than a small deficit or surplus position. Asset management, especially bonds, can now manage in concert with the term structure, duration and growth of liabilities. Ideally, short duration assets should match or outgrow short duration liabilities, intermediate and long duration assets should do the same versus the same duration liabilities. With a CLI, performance measurement can now properly compare the risk/reward behavior of any assets or total assets, versus any liabilities or total liabilities. All asset functions are now in tune with the true client objective.

Features of the Ryan ALM Custom Liability Index

The following pages show the benefits and features of the Ryan ALM Custom Liability Index, which:

1. Presents the actuarial projections of annual benefit payments and annual contributions
2. Prices and values each liability payment using ASC 715, PPA spot rates, PPA MAP-21, GASB and/or market rates (Treasury STRIPS)
3. Calculates ***present value*** for each year of the term structure with summary statistics
4. Calculates ***interest rate sensitivity*** of liabilities for each year of the term structure
5. Calculates ***growth rate*** of liabilities for each year of the term structure
6. Calculates the ***economic funded ratio*** (liability side)
7. Produces daily or monthly reports

EXHIBIT 42

Ryan ALM Custom Liability Index (Actuarial Projections)

12/31/2012

					Net	
	Future Value	Cumulative	Contributions	Cumulative	Future Value	Cumulative
12/31/2012 - 2013	20,000,000	20,000,000	2,000,000	2,000,000	18,000,000	18,000,000
12/31/2013 - 2014	20,000,000	40,000,000	2,000,000	4,000,000	18,000,000	36,000,000
12/31/2014 - 2015	20,000,000	60,000,000	2,000,000	6,000,000	18,000,000	54,000,000
12/31/2015 - 2016	20,000,000	80,000,000	2,000,000	8,000,000	18,000,000	72,000,000
12/31/2016 - 2017	20,000,000	100,000,000	2,000,000	10,000,000	18,000,000	90,000,000
12/31/2017 - 2018	20,000,000	120,000,000	2,000,000	12,000,000	18,000,000	108,000,000
12/31/2018 - 2019	20,000,000	140,000,000	2,000,000	14,000,000	18,000,000	126,000,000
12/31/2019 - 2020	20,000,000	160,000,000	2,000,000	16,000,000	18,000,000	144,000,000
12/31/2020 - 2021	20,000,000	180,000,000	2,000,000	18,000,000	18,000,000	162,000,000
12/31/2021 - 2022	20,000,000	200,000,000	2,000,000	20,000,000	18,000,000	180,000,000
12/31/2022 - 2023	20,000,000	220,000,000	1,500,000	21,500,000	18,500,000	198,500,000
12/31/2023 - 2024	20,000,000	240,000,000	1,500,000	23,000,000	18,500,000	217,000,000
12/31/2024 - 2025	20,000,000	260,000,000	1,500,000	24,500,000	18,500,000	235,500,000
12/31/2025 - 2026	20,000,000	280,000,000	1,500,000	26,000,000	18,500,000	254,000,000
12/31/2026 - 2027	20,000,000	300,000,000	1,500,000	27,500,000	18,500,000	272,500,000
12/31/2027 - 2028	20,000,000	320,000,000	1,500,000	29,000,000	18,500,000	291,000,000
12/31/2028 - 2029	20,000,000	340,000,000	1,500,000	30,500,000	18,500,000	309,500,000
12/31/2029 - 2030	20,000,000	360,000,000	1,500,000	32,000,000	18,500,000	328,000,000
12/31/2030 - 2031	20,000,000	380,000,000	1,500,000	33,500,000	18,500,000	346,500,000
12/31/2031 - 2032	20,000,000	400,000,000	1,500,000	35,000,000	18,500,000	365,000,000
12/31/2032 - 2033	20,000,000	420,000,000	1,000,000	36,000,000	19,000,000	384,000,000
12/31/2033 - 2034	20,000,000	440,000,000	1,000,000	37,000,000	19,000,000	403,000,000
12/31/2034 - 2035	20,000,000	460,000,000	1,000,000	38,000,000	19,000,000	422,000,000
12/31/2035 - 2036	20,000,000	480,000,000	1,000,000	39,000,000	19,000,000	441,000,000
12/31/2036 - 2037	20,000,000	500,000,000	1,000,000	40,000,000	19,000,000	460,000,000
12/31/2037 - 2038	20,000,000	520,000,000	1,000,000	41,000,000	19,000,000	479,000,000
12/31/2038 - 2039	20,000,000	540,000,000	1,000,000	42,000,000	19,000,000	498,000,000
12/31/2039 - 2040	20,000,000	560,000,000	1,000,000	43,000,000	19,000,000	517,000,000
12/31/2040 - 2041	20,000,000	580,000,000	1,000,000	44,000,000	19,000,000	536,000,000
12/31/2041 - 2042	20,000,000	600,000,000	1,000,000	45,000,000	19,000,000	555,000,000
Total	600,000,000	600,000,000	45,000,000	45,000,000	555,000,000	555,000,000

EXHIBIT 43

Ryan ALM Custom Liability Index
TSY STRIP - Structure
12/31/2012

Duration Cells	% Weight	# Payments	Future Value	Present Value	Averages Coupon	Price	YTW	MDUR
SHORT(0-1)	4.80	2	20,000,000	19,970,805	0.00	99.854	0.186	0.747
01.01 - 02.50	7.16	3	30,000,000	29,814,805	0.00	99.383	0.303	1.990
02.50 - 03.50	4.73	2	20,000,000	19,703,836	0.00	98.520	0.457	3.233
03.50 - 04.50	4.67	2	20,000,000	19,452,490	0.00	97.264	0.653	4.220
04.50 - 05.50	4.59	2	20,000,000	19,122,518	0.00	95.615	0.856	5.202
05.50 - 06.50	4.49	2	20,000,000	18,705,499	0.00	93.531	1.074	6.180
06.50 - 07.50	4.37	2	20,000,000	18,194,721	0.00	90.978	1.312	7.152
07.50 - 08.50	4.23	2	20,000,000	17,609,572	0.00	88.054	1.553	8.119
08.50 - 09.50	4.08	2	20,000,000	17,001,976	0.00	85.017	1.770	9.085
09.50 - 10.50	3.93	2	20,000,000	16,362,657	0.00	81.821	1.977	10.047
INTER(1- 10.50)	42.27	19	190,000,000	175,968,073	0.00	92.997	1.028	5.752
10.50 - 11.50	3.78	2	20,000,000	15,736,053	0.00	78.688	2.154	11.008
11.50 - 12.50	3.63	2	20,000,000	15,111,961	0.00	75.567	2.314	11.968
12.50 - 13.50	3.48	2	20,000,000	14,507,594	0.00	72.546	2.452	12.928
13.50 - 14.50	3.34	2	20,000,000	13,919,410	0.00	69.604	2.576	13.888
14.50 - 15.50	3.22	2	20,000,000	13,388,892	0.00	66.950	2.667	14.850
15.50 - 16.50	3.10	2	20,000,000	12,890,496	0.00	64.457	2.740	15.813
16.50 - 17.50	2.99	2	20,000,000	12,442,421	0.00	62.218	2.790	16.777
17.50 - 18.50	2.88	2	20,000,000	11,993,523	0.00	59.973	2.842	17.742
18.50 - 19.50	2.78	2	20,000,000	11,556,959	0.00	57.790	2.890	18.705
19.50 - 20.50	2.68	2	20,000,000	11,141,324	0.00	55.711	2.932	19.669
LONG(10.5 - 20.5)	31.87	20	200,000,000	132,688,633	0.00	67.156	2.609	15.031
20.50 - 21.51	2.58	2	20,000,000	10,738,156	0.00	53.696	2.970	20.633
21.50 - 22.50	2.48	2	20,000,000	10,344,171	0.00	51.725	3.008	21.596
22.50 - 23.50	2.40	2	20,000,000	10,009,291	0.00	50.051	3.022	22.564
23.50 - 24.50	2.31	2	20,000,000	9,628,506	0.00	48.147	3.061	23.526
24.50 - 25.50	2.23	2	20,000,000	9,271,996	0.00	46.364	3.092	24.489
25.50 - 26.50	2.14	2	20,000,000	8,919,792	0.00	44.603	3.124	25.450
26.50 - 27.50	2.07	2	20,000,000	8,596,877	0.00	42.987	3.147	26.415
27.50 - 28.50	1.99	2	20,000,000	8,291,869	0.00	41.463	3.166	27.379
28.50 - 29.50	1.92	2	20,000,000	7,981,363	0.00	39.909	3.191	28.342
29.50 - 30.50	0.94	1	10,000,000	3,897,402	0.00	38.974	3.191	29.072
VLONG(20.5+)	21.06	19	190,000,000	87,679,422	0.00	46.621	3.085	24.464
Total	100.00	60	600,000,000	416,306,932	0.00	75.322	1.925	12.410

EXHIBIT 44

Ryan ALM Custom Liability Index
TSY STRIP w/Contributions - Structure
12/31/2012

					Averages			
Duration Cells	% Weight	# Payments	Future Value	Present Value	Coupon	Price	YTW	MDUR
SHORT(0-1)	4.70	2	18,000,000	17,973,724	0.00	99.854	0.186	0.747
01.01 - 02.50	7.01	3	27,000,000	26,833,324	0.00	99.383	0.303	1.990
02.50 - 03.50	4.63	2	18,000,000	17,733,452	0.00	98.520	0.457	3.233
03.50 - 04.50	4.57	2	18,000,000	17,507,241	0.00	97.264	0.653	4.220
04.50 - 05.50	4.50	2	18,000,000	17,210,266	0.00	95.615	0.856	5.202
05.50 - 06.50	4.40	2	18,000,000	16,834,949	0.00	93.531	1.074	6.180
06.50 - 07.50	4.28	2	18,000,000	16,375,249	0.00	90.978	1.312	7.152
07.50 - 08.50	4.14	2	18,000,000	15,848,615	0.00	88.054	1.553	8.119
08.50 - 09.50	4.00	2	18,000,000	15,301,778	0.00	85.017	1.770	9.085
09.50 - 10.50	3.90	2	18,250,000	14,928,972	0.00	81.810	1.978	10.050
INTER(1- 10.50)	41.43	19	171,250,000	158,573,847	0.00	92.981	1.029	5.758
10.50 - 11.50	3.80	2	18,500,000	14,555,849	0.00	78.688	2.154	11.008
11.50 - 12.50	3.65	2	18,500,000	13,978,564	0.00	75.567	2.314	11.968
12.50 - 13.50	3.51	2	18,500,000	13,419,524	0.00	72.546	2.452	12.928
13.50 - 14.50	3.36	2	18,500,000	12,875,454	0.00	69.604	2.576	13.888
14.50 - 15.50	3.24	2	18,500,000	12,384,725	0.00	66.950	2.667	14.850
15.50 - 16.50	3.12	2	18,500,000	11,923,709	0.00	64.457	2.740	15.813
16.50 - 17.50	3.01	2	18,500,000	11,509,239	0.00	62.218	2.790	16.777
17.50 - 18.50	2.90	2	18,500,000	11,094,009	0.00	59.973	2.842	17.742
18.50 - 19.50	2.79	2	18,500,000	10,690,187	0.00	57.790	2.890	18.705
19.50 - 20.50	2.73	2	18,750,000	10,443,688	0.00	55.705	2.932	19.672
LONG(10.5 - 20.5)	32.11	20	185,250,000	122,874,948	0.00	67.142	2.609	15.036
20.50 - 21.51	2.67	2	19,000,000	10,201,248	0.00	53.696	2.970	20.633
21.50 - 22.50	2.57	2	19,000,000	9,826,963	0.00	51.725	3.008	21.596
22.50 - 23.50	2.48	2	19,000,000	9,508,826	0.00	50.051	3.022	22.564
23.50 - 24.50	2.39	2	19,000,000	9,147,081	0.00	48.147	3.061	23.526
24.50 - 25.50	2.30	2	19,000,000	8,808,396	0.00	46.364	3.092	24.489
25.50 - 26.50	2.21	2	19,000,000	8,473,802	0.00	44.603	3.124	25.450
26.50 - 27.50	2.13	2	19,000,000	8,167,033	0.00	42.987	3.147	26.415
27.50 - 28.50	2.06	2	19,000,000	7,877,275	0.00	41.463	3.166	27.379
28.50 - 29.50	1.98	2	19,000,000	7,582,294	0.00	39.909	3.191	28.342
29.50 - 30.50	0.97	1	9,500,000	3,702,532	0.00	38.974	3.191	29.072
VLONG(20.5+)	21.76	19	180,500,000	83,295,451	0.00	46.621	3.085	24.464
Total	100.00	60	555,000,000	382,717,970	0.00	74.918	1.944	12.573

EXHIBIT 45

Ryan ALM Custom Liability Index
Performance
12/31/2012

Duration Cells	Total Liabilities % Weight	Total Liabilities Day	Total Liabilities Month	Total Liabilities Year	Total Liabilities Index Level	With Contributions % Weight	With Contributions Day	With Contributions Month	With Contributions Year	With Contributions Index Level	Difference % Weight	Difference Day	Difference Month	Difference Year
SHORT(0-1)	4.80	-0.00	0.02	0.20	100.20	4.70	-0.00	0.02	0.20	100.20	0.10	0.00	0.00	0.00
01.01 - 02.50	7.16	0.01	0.03	0.50	100.50	7.01	0.01	0.03	0.50	100.50	0.15	0.00	0.00	0.00
02.50 - 03.50	4.73	0.02	-0.02	1.23	101.23	4.63	0.02	-0.02	1.23	101.23	0.10	0.00	0.00	0.00
03.50 - 04.50	4.67	-0.01	-0.18	1.92	101.92	4.57	-0.01	-0.18	1.92	101.92	0.10	0.00	0.00	0.00
04.50 - 05.50	4.59	-0.05	-0.31	2.80	102.80	4.50	-0.05	-0.31	2.80	102.80	0.10	0.00	0.00	0.00
05.50 - 06.50	4.49	-0.13	-0.49	3.61	103.61	4.40	-0.13	-0.49	3.61	103.61	0.09	0.00	0.00	0.00
06.50 - 07.50	4.37	-0.16	-0.64	4.54	104.54	4.28	-0.16	-0.64	4.54	104.54	0.09	0.00	0.00	0.00
07.50 - 08.50	4.23	-0.26	-0.90	5.06	105.06	4.14	-0.26	-0.90	5.06	105.06	0.09	0.00	0.00	0.00
08.50 - 09.50	4.08	-0.33	-1.06	5.40	105.40	4.00	-0.33	-1.06	5.40	105.40	0.09	-0.00	-0.00	-0.00
09.50 - 10.50	3.93	-0.41	-1.18	5.85	105.85	3.90	-0.41	-1.18	5.85	105.85	0.03	0.00	0.00	-0.00
INTER(1- 10.50)	42.27	-0.12	-0.47	3.16	103.16	41.43	-0.12	-0.47	3.16	103.16	0.84	0.00	0.00	-0.00
10.50 - 11.50	3.78	-0.51	-1.39	6.20	106.20	3.80	-0.51	-1.39	6.20	106.20	-0.02	0.00	0.00	0.00
11.50 - 12.50	3.63	-0.61	-1.61	6.26	106.26	3.65	-0.61	-1.61	6.26	106.26	-0.02	0.00	0.00	0.00
12.50 - 13.50	3.48	-0.66	-1.80	6.26	106.26	3.51	-0.66	-1.80	6.26	106.26	-0.02	0.00	0.00	0.00
13.50 - 14.50	3.34	-0.80	-2.14	5.92	105.92	3.36	-0.80	-2.14	5.92	105.92	-0.02	0.00	0.00	0.00
14.50 - 15.50	3.22	-0.86	-2.31	5.66	105.66	3.24	-0.86	-2.31	5.66	105.66	-0.02	0.00	0.00	0.00
15.50 - 16.50	3.10	-0.94	-2.46	5.33	105.33	3.12	-0.94	-2.46	5.33	105.33	-0.02	0.00	-0.00	0.00
16.50 - 17.50	2.99	-0.92	-2.49	5.23	105.23	3.01	-0.92	-2.49	5.23	105.23	-0.02	0.00	0.00	0.00
17.50 - 18.50	2.88	-1.04	-2.70	4.95	104.95	2.90	-1.04	-2.70	4.95	104.95	-0.02	0.00	0.00	0.00
18.50 - 19.50	2.78	-1.12	-2.74	4.93	104.93	2.79	-1.12	-2.74	4.93	104.93	-0.02	0.00	0.00	0.00
19.50 - 20.50	2.68	-1.13	-2.69	4.93	104.93	2.73	-1.13	-2.69	4.93	104.93	-0.05	0.00	0.00	-0.00
LONG(10.5 - 20.5)	31.87	-0.84	-2.19	5.62	105.62	32.11	-0.84	-2.19	5.62	105.62	-0.23	0.00	0.00	0.00
20.50 - 21.51	2.58	-1.16	-2.71	4.80	104.80	2.67	-1.16	-2.71	4.80	104.80	-0.09	0.00	0.00	0.00
21.50 - 22.50	2.48	-1.20	-2.74	4.85	104.85	2.57	-1.20	-2.74	4.85	104.85	-0.08	0.00	0.00	0.00
22.50 - 23.50	2.40	-1.14	-2.50	5.01	105.01	2.48	-1.14	-2.50	5.01	105.01	-0.08	0.00	0.00	0.00
23.50 - 24.50	2.31	-1.31	-2.67	4.80	104.80	2.39	-1.31	-2.67	4.80	104.80	-0.08	0.00	0.00	-0.00
24.50 - 25.50	2.23	-1.34	-2.80	4.33	104.33	2.30	-1.34	-2.80	4.33	104.33	-0.07	0.00	0.00	0.00
25.50 - 26.50	2.14	-1.56	-3.07	3.76	103.76	2.21	-1.56	-3.07	3.76	103.76	-0.07	0.00	0.00	0.00
26.50 - 27.50	2.07	-1.57	-3.06	3.02	103.02	2.13	-1.57	-3.06	3.02	103.02	-0.07	-0.00	0.00	-0.00
27.50 - 28.50	1.99	-1.64	-3.30	2.70	102.70	2.06	-1.64	-3.30	2.70	102.70	-0.07	0.00	0.00	0.00
28.50 - 29.50	1.92	-1.63	-3.49	1.96	101.96	1.98	-1.63	-3.49	1.96	101.96	-0.06	0.00	0.00	0.00
29.50 - 30.50	0.94	0.00	0.00	5.56	105.56	0.97	0.00	0.00	5.56	105.56	-0.03	0.00	0.00	0.00
VLONG(20.5+)	21.06	-1.36	-2.89	4.00	104.00	21.76	-1.36	-2.89	4.00	104.00	-0.70	0.00	0.00	0.00
Total	100.00	-0.58	-1.48	4.02	104.02	100.00	-0.59	-1.51	4.03	104.03	0.00	0.01	0.02	-0.02

EXHIBIT 46

Ryan ALM Custom Liability Index

TSY STRIP Sensitivity - Total Return Based on Interest Rate Moves over 12-Month Horizon

12/31/2012

Duration Cells	% Weight	Future Value	Present Value	YTW	MDur	100	50	-50	-100
SHORT(0-1)	4.80	20,000,000	19,970,805	0.186	0.747				
01.01 - 02.50	7.16	30,000,000	29,814,805	0.303	1.990	-0.68	-0.19	0.80	1.31
02.50 - 03.50	4.73	20,000,000	19,703,836	0.457	3.233	-1.75	-0.66	1.59	2.74
03.50 - 04.50	4.67	20,000,000	19,452,490	0.653	4.220	-2.53	-0.95	2.29	3.97
04.50 - 05.50	4.59	20,000,000	19,122,518	0.856	5.202	-3.28	-1.24	3.01	5.22
05.50 - 06.50	4.49	20,000,000	18,705,499	1.074	6.180	-4.01	-1.51	3.74	6.49
06.50 - 07.50	4.37	20,000,000	18,194,721	1.312	7.152	-4.72	-1.76	4.49	7.79
07.50 - 08.50	4.23	20,000,000	17,609,572	1.553	8.119	-5.41	-2.00	5.25	9.10
08.50 - 09.50	4.08	20,000,000	17,001,976	1.770	9.085	-6.11	-2.26	5.99	10.40
09.50 - 10.50	3.93	20,000,000	16,362,657	1.977	10.047	-6.82	-2.53	6.72	11.70
INTER(1- 10.50)	42.27	190,000,000	175,968,073	1.028	5.752	-3.63	-1.34	3.49	6.03
10.50 - 11.50	3.78	20,000,000	15,736,053	2.154	11.008	-7.55	-2.83	7.42	12.99
11.50 - 12.50	3.63	20,000,000	15,111,961	2.314	11.968	-8.29	-3.14	8.11	14.26
12.50 - 13.50	3.48	20,000,000	14,507,594	2.452	12.928	-9.04	-3.48	8.78	15.53
13.50 - 14.50	3.34	20,000,000	13,919,410	2.576	13.888	-9.79	-3.82	9.43	16.79
14.50 - 15.50	3.22	20,000,000	13,388,892	2.667	14.850	-10.57	-4.20	10.06	18.03
15.50 - 16.50	3.10	20,000,000	12,890,496	2.740	15.813	-11.36	-4.59	10.67	19.26
16.50 - 17.50	2.99	20,000,000	12,442,421	2.790	16.777	-12.17	-5.00	11.26	20.48
17.50 - 18.50	2.88	20,000,000	11,993,523	2.842	17.742	-12.96	-5.41	11.86	21.72
18.50 - 19.50	2.78	20,000,000	11,556,959	2.890	18.705	-13.76	-5.82	12.45	22.96
19.50 - 20.50	2.68	20,000,000	11,141,324	2.932	19.669	-14.54	-6.23	13.04	24.21
LONG(10.5 - 20.5)	31.87	200,000,000	132,688,633	2.609	15.031	-10.76	-4.33	10.11	18.23
20.50 - 21.51	2.58	20,000,000	10,738,156	2.970	20.633	-15.33	-6.65	13.63	25.46
21.50 - 22.50	2.48	20,000,000	10,344,171	3.008	21.596	-16.11	-7.06	14.23	26.73
22.50 - 23.50	2.40	20,000,000	10,009,291	3.022	22.564	-16.90	-7.50	14.80	27.99
23.50 - 24.50	2.31	20,000,000	9,628,506	3.061	23.526	-17.66	-7.91	15.40	29.28
24.50 - 25.50	2.23	20,000,000	9,271,996	3.092	24.489	-18.42	-8.32	15.99	30.58
25.50 - 26.50	2.14	20,000,000	8,919,792	3.124	25.450	-19.17	-8.73	16.59	31.89
26.50 - 27.50	2.07	20,000,000	8,596,877	3.147	26.415	-19.93	-9.15	17.18	33.20
27.50 - 28.50	1.99	20,000,000	8,291,869	3.166	27.379	-20.68	-9.57	17.77	34.52
28.50 - 29.50	1.92	20,000,000	7,981,363	3.191	28.342	-21.42	-9.98	18.37	35.86
29.50 - 30.50	0.94	10,000,000	3,897,402	3.191	29.072	-21.99	-10.31	18.80	36.86
VLONG(20.5+)	21.06	190,000,000	87,679,422	3.085	24.464	-18.38	-8.31	15.98	30.58
Total	100.00	600,000,000	416,306,932	1.925	12.410	-9.28	-3.88	8.47	15.55

EXHIBIT 47

Ryan ALM Custom Liability Index

TSY STRIP Sensitivity - Market Value Based on Interest Rate Moves over 12-Month Horizon

12/31/2012

Duration Cells	% Weight	Future Value	Present Value	YTW	MDur	100	50	-50	-100
SHORT(0-1)	4.80	20,000,000	19,970,805	0.186	0.747				
01.01 - 02.50	7.16	30,000,000	29,814,805	0.303	1.990	29,610,896	29,757,188	30,054,345	30,205,258
02.50 - 03.50	4.73	20,000,000	19,703,836	0.457	3.233	19,358,254	19,574,337	20,017,176	20,244,087
03.50 - 04.50	4.67	20,000,000	19,452,490	0.653	4.220	18,960,977	19,266,954	19,898,640	20,224,700
04.50 - 05.50	4.59	20,000,000	19,122,518	0.856	5.202	18,494,887	18,885,420	19,697,614	20,119,933
05.50 - 06.50	4.49	20,000,000	18,705,499	1.074	6.180	17,954,766	18,423,285	19,404,828	19,918,944
06.50 - 07.50	4.37	20,000,000	18,194,721	1.312	7.152	17,336,550	17,875,209	19,011,957	19,611,707
07.50 - 08.50	4.23	20,000,000	17,609,572	1.553	8.119	16,657,489	17,257,921	18,534,273	19,212,559
08.50 - 09.50	4.08	20,000,000	17,001,976	1.770	9.085	15,962,667	16,617,658	18,020,134	18,770,834
09.50 - 10.50	3.93	20,000,000	16,362,657	1.977	10.047	15,246,642	15,948,392	17,461,914	18,277,888
INTER(1- 10.50)	42.27	190,000,000	175,968,073	1.028	5.752	169,583,128	173,606,365	182,100,882	186,585,911
10.50 - 11.50	3.78	20,000,000	15,736,053	2.154	11.008	14,548,080	15,290,612	16,903,741	17,779,671
11.50 - 12.50	3.63	20,000,000	15,111,961	2.314	11.968	13,859,708	14,636,817	16,337,336	17,267,346
12.50 - 13.50	3.48	20,000,000	14,507,594	2.452	12.928	13,196,630	14,003,203	15,781,034	16,760,296
13.50 - 14.50	3.34	20,000,000	13,919,410	2.576	13.888	12,556,260	13,387,386	15,232,667	16,256,362
14.50 - 15.50	3.22	20,000,000	13,388,892	2.667	14.850	11,973,071	12,826,757	14,735,971	15,802,733
15.50 - 16.50	3.10	20,000,000	12,890,496	2.740	15.813	11,425,545	12,298,880	14,266,325	15,373,512
16.50 - 17.50	2.99	20,000,000	12,442,421	2.790	16.777	10,928,220	11,820,049	13,843,896	14,991,008
17.50 - 18.50	2.88	20,000,000	11,993,523	2.842	17.742	10,438,607	11,344,667	13,415,897	14,598,288
18.50 - 19.50	2.78	20,000,000	11,556,959	2.890	18.705	9,967,296	10,884,406	12,996,282	14,210,513
19.50 - 20.50	2.68	20,000,000	11,141,324	2.932	19.669	9,520,874	10,446,802	12,594,650	13,838,410
LONG(10.5 - 20.5)	31.87	200,000,000	132,688,633	2.609	15.031	118,414,291	126,939,578	146,107,800	156,878,137
20.50 - 21.51	2.58	20,000,000	10,738,156	2.970	20.633	9,092,128	10,024,219	12,202,262	13,472,531
21.50 - 22.50	2.48	20,000,000	10,344,171	3.008	21.596	8,678,095	9,613,626	11,815,790	13,109,306
22.50 - 23.50	2.40	20,000,000	10,009,291	3.022	22.564	8,317,854	9,258,912	11,490,462	12,810,637
23.50 - 24.50	2.31	20,000,000	9,628,506	3.061	23.526	7,928,102	8,867,321	11,110,893	12,447,637
24.50 - 25.50	2.23	20,000,000	9,271,996	3.092	24.489	7,563,974	8,500,614	10,754,522	12,106,996
25.50 - 26.50	2.14	20,000,000	8,919,792	3.124	25.450	7,209,577	8,141,125	10,399,295	11,763,964
26.50 - 27.50	2.07	20,000,000	8,596,877	3.147	26.415	6,883,757	7,810,505	10,073,641	11,451,054
27.50 - 28.50	1.99	20,000,000	8,291,869	3.166	27.379	6,577,298	7,498,604	9,765,094	11,154,369
28.50 - 29.50	1.92	20,000,000	7,981,363	3.191	28.342	6,272,109	7,184,934	9,447,165	10,843,678
29.50 - 30.50	0.94	10,000,000	3,897,402	3.191	29.072	3,040,553	3,495,730	4,630,094	5,334,114
VLONG(20.5+)	21.06	190,000,000	87,679,422	3.085	24.464	71,563,446	80,395,590	101,689,217	114,494,286
Total	100.00	600,000,000	416,306,932	1.925	12.410	359,560,865	380,941,533	429,897,898	457,958,334

"Use the wrong index, you will get the wrong risk/reward. It's that simple."

—Ronald J. Ryan, CFA

CHAPTER **THIRTEEN**

PENSION SOLUTION: CONTRIBUTIONS

Pension contributions are a future asset. As a result, they enhance the funded ratio. Usually such contributions are paid in the form of cash and are used to fund that year's liability payments. Should the contribution be larger than what is required for that fiscal year, it would be used for the next fiscal year(s). Accordingly, **current pension assets are required to fund the *net* liabilities (after contributions) and not the *gross* liabilities (before contributions).** Asset allocation and asset management should be acutely aware of this fact. It is rare to see the *net* funded ratio (after contributions are paid) ever calculated or used in any asset decision.

When used to fund liabilities, contributions reduce liabilities thereby enhancing the future funded ratio. Anything that affects the funded ratio should also affect the asset allocation decision. Anything that affects the funded ratio and the custom liability index (CLI) should also affect asset management and performance measurement...it all links! The Ryan ALM Custom Liability Index is calculated to provide all reports based on both *gross* liabilities (before contributions) and *net* liabilities (after contributions).

The *net* CLI would not only be a lower liability future value and lower present value, but also usually a longer duration. This would also increase interest rate risk and the volatility of liability present values. Exhibit 48 highlights the summary statistics calculated from the CLI in Exhibits 43, 44 and 50 where we assume actuarial projections, including annual contributions of $2 million per year for the first 10 years, $1.5 million for the next 10 years, and then $1 million per year for the last 10 years on liability payments of $20 million per year (Exhibit 49). Such a rather small contribution (9% of liability payments) also reduces present value (PV) by 9%.

EXHIBIT 48

GROSS LIABILITIES PRESENT VALUE (PV) VS. NET LIABILITIES PV

Gross PV	MDuration	Net PV	MDuration
$416,306,932	12.41 years	$382,717,378	12.57 years

In reality, the annual required contributions (ARCs) are very high and volatile today. When paid in full, contributions can dramatically reduce the present value of liabilities, but will also lengthen modified duration, making liabilities more interest rate sensitive. Whatever the plan sponsor feels is a comfortable budget for contributions should be the target. So either the annual required contribution (ARC) or the target contribution should be used to create a net liability schedule that current assets will fund.

It is an ominous trend that in the last 13 years up to 2012, contributions have grown steadily, (perhaps even spiking), starting with the equity correction period of 2000 to 2002, and escalating from there. For many pensions the minimum required contribution costs are quite significant. However, these contribution payments could greatly reduce liabilities, thereby enhancing funded ratios, altering asset allocation decisions, changing the way assets are managed (mainly bonds matched to liabilities) and ultimately changing the results of performance measurement reports (asset growth versus net liability growth) in a positive way.

EXHIBIT 49

Ryan ALM Custom Liability Index (Actuarial Projections)

12/31/2012

	Future Value	Cumulative	Contributions	Cumulative	Net Future Value	Net Cumulative
12/31/2012 - 2013	20,000,000	20,000,000	2,000,000	2,000,000	18,000,000	18,000,000
12/31/2013 - 2014	20,000,000	40,000,000	2,000,000	4,000,000	18,000,000	36,000,000
12/31/2014 - 2015	20,000,000	60,000,000	2,000,000	6,000,000	18,000,000	54,000,000
12/31/2015 - 2016	20,000,000	80,000,000	2,000,000	8,000,000	18,000,000	72,000,000
12/31/2016 - 2017	20,000,000	100,000,000	2,000,000	10,000,000	18,000,000	90,000,000
12/31/2017 - 2018	20,000,000	120,000,000	2,000,000	12,000,000	18,000,000	108,000,000
12/31/2018 - 2019	20,000,000	140,000,000	2,000,000	14,000,000	18,000,000	126,000,000
12/31/2019 - 2020	20,000,000	160,000,000	2,000,000	16,000,000	18,000,000	144,000,000
12/31/2020 - 2021	20,000,000	180,000,000	2,000,000	18,000,000	18,000,000	162,000,000
12/31/2021 - 2022	20,000,000	200,000,000	2,000,000	20,000,000	18,000,000	180,000,000
12/31/2022 - 2023	20,000,000	220,000,000	1,500,000	21,500,000	18,500,000	198,500,000
12/31/2023 - 2024	20,000,000	240,000,000	1,500,000	23,000,000	18,500,000	217,000,000
12/31/2024 - 2025	20,000,000	260,000,000	1,500,000	24,500,000	18,500,000	235,500,000
12/31/2025 - 2026	20,000,000	280,000,000	1,500,000	26,000,000	18,500,000	254,000,000
12/31/2026 - 2027	20,000,000	300,000,000	1,500,000	27,500,000	18,500,000	272,500,000
12/31/2027 - 2028	20,000,000	320,000,000	1,500,000	29,000,000	18,500,000	291,000,000
12/31/2028 - 2029	20,000,000	340,000,000	1,500,000	30,500,000	18,500,000	309,500,000
12/31/2029 - 2030	20,000,000	360,000,000	1,500,000	32,000,000	18,500,000	328,000,000
12/31/2030 - 2031	20,000,000	380,000,000	1,500,000	33,500,000	18,500,000	346,500,000
12/31/2031 - 2032	20,000,000	400,000,000	1,500,000	35,000,000	18,500,000	365,000,000
12/31/2032 - 2033	20,000,000	420,000,000	1,000,000	36,000,000	19,000,000	384,000,000
12/31/2033 - 2034	20,000,000	440,000,000	1,000,000	37,000,000	19,000,000	403,000,000
12/31/2034 - 2035	20,000,000	460,000,000	1,000,000	38,000,000	19,000,000	422,000,000
12/31/2035 - 2036	20,000,000	480,000,000	1,000,000	39,000,000	19,000,000	441,000,000
12/31/2036 - 2037	20,000,000	500,000,000	1,000,000	40,000,000	19,000,000	460,000,000
12/31/2037 - 2038	20,000,000	520,000,000	1,000,000	41,000,000	19,000,000	479,000,000
12/31/2038 - 2039	20,000,000	540,000,000	1,000,000	42,000,000	19,000,000	498,000,000
12/31/2039 - 2040	20,000,000	560,000,000	1,000,000	43,000,000	19,000,000	517,000,000
12/31/2040 - 2041	20,000,000	580,000,000	1,000,000	44,000,000	19,000,000	536,000,000
12/31/2041 - 2042	20,000,000	600,000,000	1,000,000	45,000,000	19,000,000	555,000,000
Total	600,000,000	600,000,000	45,000,000	45,000,000	555,000,000	555,000,000

EXHIBIT 50

Ryan ALM Custom Liability Index with Contributions
TSY STRIP - Structure
12/31/2012

Duration Cells	% Weight	# Payments	Future Value	Present Value	Averages Coupon	Price	YTW	MDUR
SHORT(0-1)	4.70	2	18,000,000	17,973,724	0.00	99.854	0.186	0.747
01.01 - 02.50	7.01	3	27,000,000	26,833,324	0.00	99.383	0.303	1.990
02.50 - 03.50	4.63	2	18,000,000	17,733,452	0.00	98.520	0.457	3.233
03.50 - 04.50	4.57	2	18,000,000	17,507,241	0.00	97.264	0.653	4.220
04.50 - 05.50	4.50	2	18,000,000	17,210,266	0.00	95.615	0.856	5.202
05.50 - 06.50	4.40	2	18,000,000	16,834,949	0.00	93.531	1.074	6.180
06.50 - 07.50	4.28	2	18,000,000	16,375,249	0.00	90.978	1.312	7.152
07.50 - 08.50	4.14	2	18,000,000	15,848,615	0.00	88.054	1.553	8.119
08.50 - 09.50	4.00	2	18,000,000	15,301,778	0.00	85.017	1.770	9.085
09.50 - 10.50	3.90	2	18,250,000	14,928,972	0.00	81.810	1.978	10.050
INTER(1- 10.50)	41.43	19	171,250,000	158,573,847	0.00	92.981	1.029	5.758
10.50 - 11.50	3.80	2	18,500,000	14,555,849	0.00	78.688	2.154	11.008
11.50 - 12.50	3.65	2	18,500,000	13,978,564	0.00	75.567	2.314	11.968
12.50 - 13.50	3.51	2	18,500,000	13,419,524	0.00	72.546	2.452	12.928
13.50 - 14.50	3.36	2	18,500,000	12,875,454	0.00	69.604	2.576	13.888
14.50 - 15.50	3.24	2	18,500,000	12,384,725	0.00	66.950	2.667	14.850
15.50 - 16.50	3.12	2	18,500,000	11,923,709	0.00	64.457	2.740	15.813
16.50 - 17.50	3.01	2	18,500,000	11,509,239	0.00	62.218	2.790	16.777
17.50 - 18.50	2.90	2	18,500,000	11,094,009	0.00	59.973	2.842	17.742
18.50 - 19.50	2.79	2	18,500,000	10,690,187	0.00	57.790	2.890	18.705
19.50 - 20.50	2.73	2	18,750,000	10,443,688	0.00	55.705	2.932	19.672
LONG(10.5 - 20.5)	32.11	20	185,250,000	122,874,948	0.00	67.142	2.609	15.036
20.50 - 21.51	2.67	2	19,000,000	10,201,248	0.00	53.696	2.970	20.633
21.50 - 22.50	2.57	2	19,000,000	9,826,963	0.00	51.725	3.008	21.596
22.50 - 23.50	2.48	2	19,000,000	9,508,826	0.00	50.051	3.022	22.564
23.50 - 24.50	2.39	2	19,000,000	9,147,081	0.00	48.147	3.061	23.526
24.50 - 25.50	2.30	2	19,000,000	8,808,396	0.00	46.364	3.092	24.489
25.50 - 26.50	2.21	2	19,000,000	8,473,802	0.00	44.603	3.124	25.450
26.50 - 27.50	2.13	2	19,000,000	8,167,033	0.00	42.987	3.147	26.415
27.50 - 28.50	2.06	2	19,000,000	7,877,275	0.00	41.463	3.166	27.379
28.50 - 29.50	1.98	2	19,000,000	7,582,294	0.00	39.909	3.191	28.342
29.50 - 30.50	0.97	1	9,500,000	3,702,532	0.00	38.974	3.191	29.072
VLONG(20.5+)	21.76	19	180,500,000	83,295,451	0.00	46.621	3.085	24.464
Total	100.00	60	555,000,000	382,717,970	0.00	74.918	1.944	12.573

"How blind we are to the obvious."

—Tom McMahon

CHAPTER **FOURTEEN**

PENSION SOLUTION: ASSET ALLOCATION

The goal of *traditional* asset allocation has been to create the optimal *absolute return* (ROA). Such models use historical generic market index data (20+ years). As a result, stocks have been favored consistently. However, the true objective of asset allocation should be to create the optimal *relative return* versus liabilities (liability alpha). **Until a *custom* liability index (CLI) is installed as the proper benchmark, all asset allocation, asset management, benefit, and contribution decisions will be made based upon erroneous and misleading calculations...it all links!** Asset allocation is usually the first asset decision as well as the most important since it affects all assets. **Asset allocation should be based on the *economic* funded ratio and not the ROA!** The CLI will calculate the market value of liabilities, such that the true economic funded ratio will now be known frequently and accurately. This will allow asset allocation to function in harmony with the true liability objective. In order to achieve proper asset allocation, we need to better define or redefine certain key terms:

Alpha

Alpha is the excess return versus the objective return. With a liability objective, liability alpha is the excess asset growth versus liability growth as measured by the CLI. When assets outperform a generic market index, yet underperform liability growth, it is market alpha, but it is not considered liability alpha.

Alpha Assets

Alpha assets are the performance assets (i.e., non-bonds) that are expected to outgrow liability growth.

Beta Assets

Beta assets are the assets that match the risk/reward of the objective (e.g., high quality zero-coupon bonds that match the CLI risk/reward behavior).

Liability Beta

With a liability objective, liability beta is the portfolio (or liability index fund) that matches the liability risk/reward behavior. Assets that match a generic market index is *market* beta, but is not *liability* beta. Equities in any form (e.g., S&P 500 index fund) could never match liabilities and could never qualify as a liability beta portfolio.

A funded ratio *surplus* should suggest a conservative asset allocation to secure this victory and reduce contribution costs long term. In the 1990s, most pension plans had steadily improving funded ratios with growing surpluses. By 1999, many pension plans were overfunded on an economic, or market value, basis with funded ratios above 120%. A 120% funded ratio should have been immunized with a *core* portfolio of bonds *matched to liabilities* (liability beta portfolio) for most of the assets (at 83% or 100%/120%) with a separate surplus portfolio created for the excess funds (at 17%) as a reserve against actuarial noise in their projections. **Had pension plan sponsors matched liabilities in the late 1990s, they would have avoided the disasters that followed: spiking contribution costs, budget deficits**

(for cities and states), EPS drag, credit rating downgrades, and of course, the $4 trillion pension deficit!

Unfortunately, pension plan sponsors have been brainwashed or misled by accounting rules to focus on the ROA as the target return of pension assets. In 1982, as interest rates began to fall in a secular trend, most pension bond allocations were reduced, especially around 1990 when yields went below the ROA, thereby suggesting that bonds could not validate or achieve the ROA. As a result, by 1999, most pension plans had the lowest allocation to bonds (and the highest allocation to equities) in modern history. When the equity correction hit in 2000 to 2002, it hurt twice as much because (1) most equities underperformed liability growth by over -70%, and (2) because of the heavy asset allocation tilt to equities. This all could have been avoided with an asset/liability matching strategy (i.e., liability beta portfolio). Even though bond yields were below the ROA, no contributions would have been necessary if there were a true *economic* funded ratio surplus (as explained in Chapter 6 in Exhibit 18, and repeated in Exhibit 51 on the next page). This may not be the case for overfunded funded ratios based on GASB and PPA (three segment discount rates) funding valuations, since the surplus calculations are not economically accurate (due to smoothing and higher than market discount rates). In these cases, there may be a true *economic* deficit with a reported *accounting* surplus.

EXHIBIT 51 (COPY OF EXHIBIT 18)

EXAMPLE: FUNDED RATIO = 140% (40% SURPLUS)						
	Growth Rate = 8% ROA				Contributions	
Year	**Assets**	**$ Growth**	**Liabilities**	**$ Growth**	**$ Cost**	**% Increase**
1	$100.00	$8.00	$71.43	$5.71	$NA	
2	108.00	8.64	77.14	6.18	NA	
3	116.64	9.33	83.32	6.66	NA	
4	125.97	10.07	89.98	7.20	NA	
5	136.05	10.88	97.18	7.77	NA	
6	146.93	11.72	104.95	8.40	NA	

Requires an ROA = 5.72% for NO Contribution costs
Assets < Liability growth by -2.28% = NO Contribution

A funded ratio *deficit* should suggest a more aggressive asset allocation. The bigger the percent deficit, the more aggressive the asset allocation should tilt towards liability alpha assets. With a CLI, we can measure the annual target liability alpha (excess asset growth versus liability growth) needed for pension assets to reach a fully funded status over the average life, or duration, of the pension. Moreover, you can measure or calculate the appropriate allocation to alpha assets (performance assets to outgrow liabilities) versus beta assets (bonds matched to liabilities). **The annual target liability alpha should replace the ROA as the target asset growth rate!** The annual target liability alpha is a *relative* excess return calculation. As a result, it is dynamic and responsive to each pension's unique funded ratio situation. The annual target liability alpha (Exhibits 52 and 53) shows pension plan sponsors and their consultants how much the pension assets need to outgrow liability growth each year in order to reach a fully funded status over the duration, or average life, of the liabilities.

EXHIBIT 52

ANNUAL TARGET LIABILITY ALPHA (REQUIRED TO REACH FULL FUNDING OVER 10 YEAR DURATION)			
A Funded Ratio	B Deficit %	C Modified Duration	D Annual Target Alpha (B/A) / C
50%	50%	10 years	10.00%
60%	40%	10 years	6.67%
70%	30%	10 years	4.29%
80%	20%	10 years	2.50%

As shown above, a pension plan with a 50% funded ratio and a duration of 10 years must have its pension assets outgrow liabilities by 10% per year in dollars (liability alpha) on average to reach a fully funded status in 10 years, while a pension plan with an 80% funded ratio requires liability alpha of only 2.50% per year. The longer the duration, the more time pension assets have to create liability alpha. This increase in duration from 10 to 15 years (shown in Exhibit 53) reduces the amount of annual liability alpha that is needed to reach full funding over the time horizon.

EXHIBIT 53

ANNUAL TARGET LIABILITY ALPHA (REQUIRED TO REACH FULL FUNDING OVER 15-YEAR DURATION)			
A Funded Ratio	B Deficit %	C Modified Duration	D Annual Target Alpha (B/A) / C
50%	50%	15 years	6.67%
60%	40%	15 years	4.44%
70%	30%	15 years	2.86%
80%	20%	15 years	1.67%

It should be apparent that the funded ratio is dictating the amount of liability alpha that is needed, which should also dictate the type of asset allocation that is appropriate. A static absolute return target (ROA) would certainly not be responsive to the changing funded ratio and would dictate an inappropriate and rather static asset allocation. The disastrous performance of pensions during the decade of 2000 only supports the obvious need to revalue the credibility of using the ROA as a target return.

Please note that there are three ways that a pension can earn the annual target liability alpha that is needed to reach full funding:

1. **The assets grow well, earning or exceeding the liability alpha annual target.**
2. **The liabilities have poor or negative growth due to rising interest rates.**
3. **Both growth trends stated in 1 and 2 above, occur.**

Since many economists and investment professionals believe that interest rates must trend upward over the next five years, let's take a look at how this scenario can significantly affect pension funded ratios if assets outgrow liabilities (liability alpha) and thus affect asset allocation (see Exhibit 54).

EXHIBIT 54

LIABILITY ALPHA ENHANCES FUNDED RATIO

Assumptions: 5-year Horizon
Interest Rates go UP over 5 years = +60 bps per year = 300 bps
10-year Treasury STRIPS = 1.92% (12/31/12) > 4.92% (12/31/17)
15-year Treasury STRIPS = 2.63% (12/31/12) > 5.63% (12/31/17)

	CLI Modified Duration = 15 years Annual Growth Rates			
Assets	5.00%	6.00%	7.00%	8.00%
Liabilities	- 6.70%	- 6.70%	- 6.70%	- 6.70%
Liability Alpha	11.70%	12.70%	13.70%	14.70%
Funded Ratio (start at)	**Ending Funded Ratios**			
50% >	90%	94%	99%	104%
60% >	108%	113%	119%	124%
70% >	126%	132%	139%	145%

	CLI Modified Duration = 10 years Annual Growth Rates			
Assets	5.00%	6.00%	7.00%	8.00%
Liabilities	- 3.08%	- 3.08%	- 3.08%	- 3.08%
Liability Alpha	8.08%	9.08%	10.08%	11.08%
Funded Ratio (start at)	**Ending Funded Ratios**			
50% >	75%	78%	82%	86%
60% >	90%	94%	98%	103%
70% >	104%	110%	115%	120%

Amazingly, a pension plan with a 60% funded ratio and a 10- to 15-year liability duration can reach a fully funded status in only five years. That is, if assets have some positive growth (5%), and interest rates climb +300 basis points over five years, such that 10-year Treasury STRIPS yield around 4.92% (from 1.92% as of Dec. 31, 2012) and 15-year Treasury STRIPS yield 5.63% (from 2.63% as of Dec. 31, 2012). Even if assets grow below the ROA rate (at 8% for most pensions), pension funded ratios would be fully funded in five years, starting at levels of 60% and greater. Achieving true economic liability alpha is the fastest and lowest risk way to achieve a fully funded status. The focus here is on the funded ratio and not on the ROA or an absolute return goal. Hopefully, the financial message is clear here:

Logic: You do NOT need to earn the ROA to achieve a fully funded status and reduce contribution costs. You need assets to outgrow liabilities (liability alpha)!

A low or declining economic funded ratio would require a more aggressive asset allocation to make up the deficit over time. Fortunately, pensions have time to cure their deficits equal to the average life (modified duration) of their liabilities. This is best measured by the CLI. Most pensions have a duration between 10 and 15 years. The pension growth rate objective should be a positive relative asset growth rate difference versus liability growth (alpha) and not an absolute growth rate (ROA). With the CLI in place, (similar to a scoreboard in sports), the pension plan sponsor (i.e., the coach) can now adjust the asset allocation whenever the funded ratio (score) indicates it's time to do so. The sports team that is way ahead will change its strategy and get conservative (and vice versa when it is way behind) — all based on the relative score versus their opponent (liability growth as measured by the CLI). What was missing all these years was a scoreboard (i.e., the CLI) measuring assets versus liabilities continually and accurately.

Logic: Assets have to outgrow liabilities to enhance the funded ratio (not earn the ROA rate).

With the CLI in place and the economic funded ratio now measured accurately and regularly, we can now calculate an appropriate asset allocation in harmony with the liability objective. The initial asset allocation step should be to focus on the amount of liability alpha assets needed to reach full funding over the duration of liabilities. This means a distinct and separate allocation of the liability alpha assets away from the liability beta assets. This allocation between the liability beta and alpha assets is based on the economic funded ratio and time (duration). The lower the funded ratio and the shorter the duration, the more is allocated to the alpha assets (and vice versa). The yield to maturity (YTM) of liabilities is their growth rate to maturity. As a result, we know the true economic growth of our liability objective to each of its payment dates (i.e., a yield curve of discount rates). If we use the YTM of the CLI as the liabilities average growth rate to their average life (duration), we can measure the allocation to liability alpha assets, with the allocation to liability beta assets as the reciprocal from this asset allocation process.

In Exhibit 53, we use the Ryan ALM Asset Allocation Model (RAAM) for an example of a pension with a market value of assets of $500 million and liabilities of $1 billion (a 50% funded ratio). As discussed in Chapter 11, I urge that contributions be considered as a future asset and a liability reduction. We assume future contributions of $10 million per year or $300 million future value. We subtract the present value of these contributions to calculate the net liability. As a result of contributions, the funded ratio is now enhanced (60%). As the RAAM model shows, this leaves a deficit of $333,333,334 to be erased over the average life of liabilities (duration = 15 years). Given the ROA of assets, we have an estimated asset growth rate of 8%, and given the YTM of the CLI, we have an estimated growth rate of liabilities of 4%. Subtracting the two rates suggests an estimated liability alpha of 4% per year. We must now compare the estimated asset alpha to what is required to reach full funding over the duration of liabilities (15 years). Dividing the deficit (40%) by the funded ratio (60%) gives us the cumulative liability alpha needed (66.7%). We then divide this cumulative liability alpha by the duration of the CLI (15 years) to get the annual target liability alpha of 4.44% per year.

With this information we now process the appropriate allocation to alpha assets. Dividing the annual target liability alpha of 4.44% by the estimated liability alpha of 4% (line 12) gives us an answer of 111% allocation to alpha assets. This is naturally "mission impossible," and suggests that even a 100% allocation will still not reach a full funding status in 15 years if assets grow at 8% and liabilities grow at 4%. We need assets to outgrow liabilities by 4.44% per year, not 4%.

Let's create a five-year scenario (illustrated in Exhibit 55). The assumptions are that assets only grow at 6%, but liabilities grow at **-2.6%** annually due to interest rates going up 60 bps per year from 4% to 7% on the YTM of liabilities. Now, let's examine what happens. In just five short years, we are now close to fully funded (line 7 = 95.90%). Applying this asset allocation model math shows a dramatic change in the allocation between liability alpha and beta assets from 100% alpha initially, to 34.20% in five years. This is dynamic (tactical) and responsive asset allocation to the changing funded ratio. If the plan becomes overfunded, then we allocate enough to the liability beta assets to fund 100% of liabilities. Then, no matter what the liability beta portfolio yield is, it should match liability growth. Alpha assets then become a reserve or surplus portfolio to protect against any actuarial noise or changing liabilities due to unforeseen actuarial estimates.

Any surplus could be isolated into a separate portfolio (similar to the NAIC rules for insurance companies) and given a different objective. Such an objective could be to outgrow inflation, which

EXHIBIT 55

RYAN ALM ASSET ALLOCATION MODEL (RAAM) ALL RIGHTS RESERVED 2011 (PATENT PENDING)			
		Current	5 years Later
1. Market Value of Assets	$	500,000,000	669,112,789
2. Market Value of Liabilities	$	1,000,000,000	823,374,138
3. Funded Ratio	%	50.0	81.3
4. Surplus (Deficit)	$	(333,333,334)	(154,261,349)
5. Contributions (Present Value)	$	166,666,666	125,640,000
6. *Net* Liabilities (-Contributions)	$	833,333,334	697,734,138
7. *Net* Funded Ratio	%	60.0	95.90
8. *Net* Surplus (Deficit)	%	(40.0)	(4.10)
9. *Net* Surplus (Deficit)	$	(333,333,334)	
10. Projected ROA	%	8.00	8.00
11. Yield of Custom Liability Index	%	4.00	7.00
12. Projected Liability Alpha (9-10)	%	4.00	1.00
13. Modified Duration	YRS	15.00	12.50
14. Annual Target Alpha (8/7)/13	%	4.44	0.34
15. Alpha Portfolios (Non-bonds)	%	100.0	34.20
16. Beta Portfolio (Bonds)	%	00.0	65.80

Assets: grow at 6% (Actual), Projected ROA = 8.00%
Liabilities: grow at -3.7% (annual), CLI yield goes up 60 bps annually
Contributions: $10 million per year x 30 years = $300 million (FV)
Modified Duration of Liabilities = 15 years (Line 13)

would protect or enhance benefits. If large enough and secured by the beta portfolio, such a surplus could be used to fund OPEB benefits.

The financial moral of our illustration is once again to focus on the economic funded ratio and outgrowing liabilities. The ROA is not the appropriate objective or focus and will mislead pension plan sponsors and their consultants into inappropriate asset allocation decisions. A CLI will provide the necessary information on liabilities to ascertain the annual target liability alpha needed to reach full funding over the average life of liabilities (modified duration). This time horizon can also be changed to best fit each client. With a CLI installed as the true objective or focus, asset allocation and the funded ratio can now be monitored at every asset review meeting. Accurate funded ratio and liability growth calculations can now be reviewed monthly to replace the annual and even triennial practices that use very delinquent data. Had pension plan sponsors and their consultants employed such a dynamic, tactical and responsive asset allocation in the late 1990s, they would have avoided all of the contribution costs, credit rating problems and the $4 trillion of pension deficits they now face.

Asset allocation goal:
Enhance the funded ratio by assets outgrowing liabilities, not by assets growing at the ROA rate.

"Insanity is doing the same thing over and over again and expecting different results."

—Albert Einstein

CHAPTER **FIFTEEN**

PENSION SOLUTION: ASSET/LIABILITY MANAGEMENT (ALM)

The sole objective of most institutional assets in America is to fund some type of liability schedule. Defined benefit pension funds are a multi-trillion dollar industry[55] with the required purpose of properly funding the pension benefit payment schedule. The number of lotteries has increased in the U.S., with over 30 states enjoying income while fulfilling their obligation to pay a well-defined liability payment schedule. Nuclear decommissioning trusts were created for the single objective of funding a distinct liability schedule out into the distant future. Debt service funds are built for the singular objective of funding principal and interest payments on a distinct liability payment schedule. Insurance companies sell annuities, GICs and other guaranteed income products which become liabilities that have to be funded properly. Post-retirement medical benefits (OPEB) are the new liabilities of tomorrow that provide many private corporations and public plans with the daunting challenge of how to fund such a large and fast growing liability schedule. Social Security and Medicare may be the millstone around our country's financial neck, forcing us to learn how to finance prudently such a massive liability expense. And there

55 *Pensions & Investments*, Survey (Sept. 30, 2009).

are many more distinct liability objectives. In America, the growth and behavior of the liability objective will determine the future behavior of all the assets that are positioned to fund such liabilities.

As dominant as liabilities are as the primary objective of so much of America's structure, asset/liability management (ALM) seems to take a back seat to other financial objectives such as beat the market, ROA, and performance within peer groups. I see this absence of ALM as one of the consequences of improper accounting rules—such that the liability objective is seldom made accurate and transparent as an index so asset/liability management becomes difficult to execute. For this reason, I devoted Chapter 12 to demonstrating the fact that the most accurate *economic* valuation (market value) of liabilities is through the installation of a custom liability index (CLI). Using a CLI is the first step in prudent and proper asset/liability management. Apparently, the Society of Actuaries (SOA) agrees.

Society of Actuaries (SOA)

The Society of Actuaries Task Force on Asset Liability Management Principles in its October 2004 exposure draft argued that to properly manage assets versus liabilities (ALM), we need to focus on economic valuations (market valuations) and not accounting valuations. The Task Force stated succinctly in Section III, Principles, A. Economic Value:

> *A consistent ALM structure can only be achieved for economic objectives. Economic value is based on future assets and liability cash flows. ALM uses these future cash flows to determine the risk exposure and achieve the financial objectives of an entity. An entity's financial objectives may include maximizing one or more of these values: economic value, accounting measures such as earnings and return on equity, or embedded value. For private pension plans, financial objectives may include the pattern of fu-*

ture funding requirements. Various accounting measures are affected by rules that change the emergence of income and the reported book value of assets and liabilities. These measures can sometimes distort economic reality and produce results inconsistent with economic value. Because ALM is concerned with the future asset and liability cash flows, the natural focus of ALM is ***economic value****. Accounting measures or future funding requirements are often included as constraints within an ALM framework. Entities that focus on economic value tend to achieve their financial objectives more consistently in the long run.*[56]

The Task Force went on in Section IV, Considerations to say:

In practice many entities do not focus on economic value and focus instead on accounting earnings...

However, ALM is internally consistent only if it is based on economic value...

If an entity is not concerned with economic value, it does not need ALM. However, many entities who have managed their assets and liabilities based on the accounting treatment ended up mismatching their assets and liabilities and ultimately failed.[57]

As explained in the last chapter, asset allocation is the first and most important asset decision. It should separate assets into liability beta and liability alpha portfolios as distinct asset management profiles. Each portfolio grouping has its own clear mission statement.

56 Task Force on Asset Liability Management Principles, *Principles Underlying Asset Liability Management* (Schaumburg, IL: Society of Actuaries, Oct. 12, 2004).

57 Ibid.

Liability *Alpha* Portfolios

The mission of the alpha portfolio(s) is to outgrow liabilities (as measured by the CLI) and enhance the funded ratio. As mentioned previously, alpha is defined as the excess return above the index objective's return. In liability driven objectives, **alpha is correctly measured as the excess return above liability growth (as measured by the CLI).** Unfortunately most pension assets are managed versus *generic* market indexes or the ROA. Outperforming generic indexes and the ROA is an inappropriate mission, and not in harmony with the true pension liability objective. The facts are clear from historical performance trends. **If you outperform a generic market index but lose to liability growth (CLI): You lose!** The infamous "correction years" for the stock market (2000 through 2002) certainly highlight this alpha clarification. As hard as it is to believe, the S&P 500 underperformed an equally weighted Treasury STRIPS portfolio with a 12.5-year average duration (Ryan Liability Benchmark Index) by **-75.88%** over those three years as displayed in Exhibit 56 below.

EXHIBIT 56

S&P 500 VS. RYAN LIABILITY BENCHMARK INDEX (ANNUAL RETURNS)

	2000	2001	2002	Cumulative
S&P 500 Index	- 9.09	11.86	- 22.08	- 20.76%
Ryan Liability Benchmark Index	25.96	3.08	19.47	55.12
				- 75.88%

Ryan Liability = equal weighting of 1-30 year Ryan STRIPS indexes

In the last 10 years ending Dec. 31, 2012, it is hard to find a single asset class outside of bonds that outperforms liabilities as measured by the Ryan Liability Benchmark Index (1-30 year Ryan Treasury STRIPS yield curve indexes equally weighted). The graph in Exhibit 57 shows a comparison of the popular generic market

EXHIBIT 57

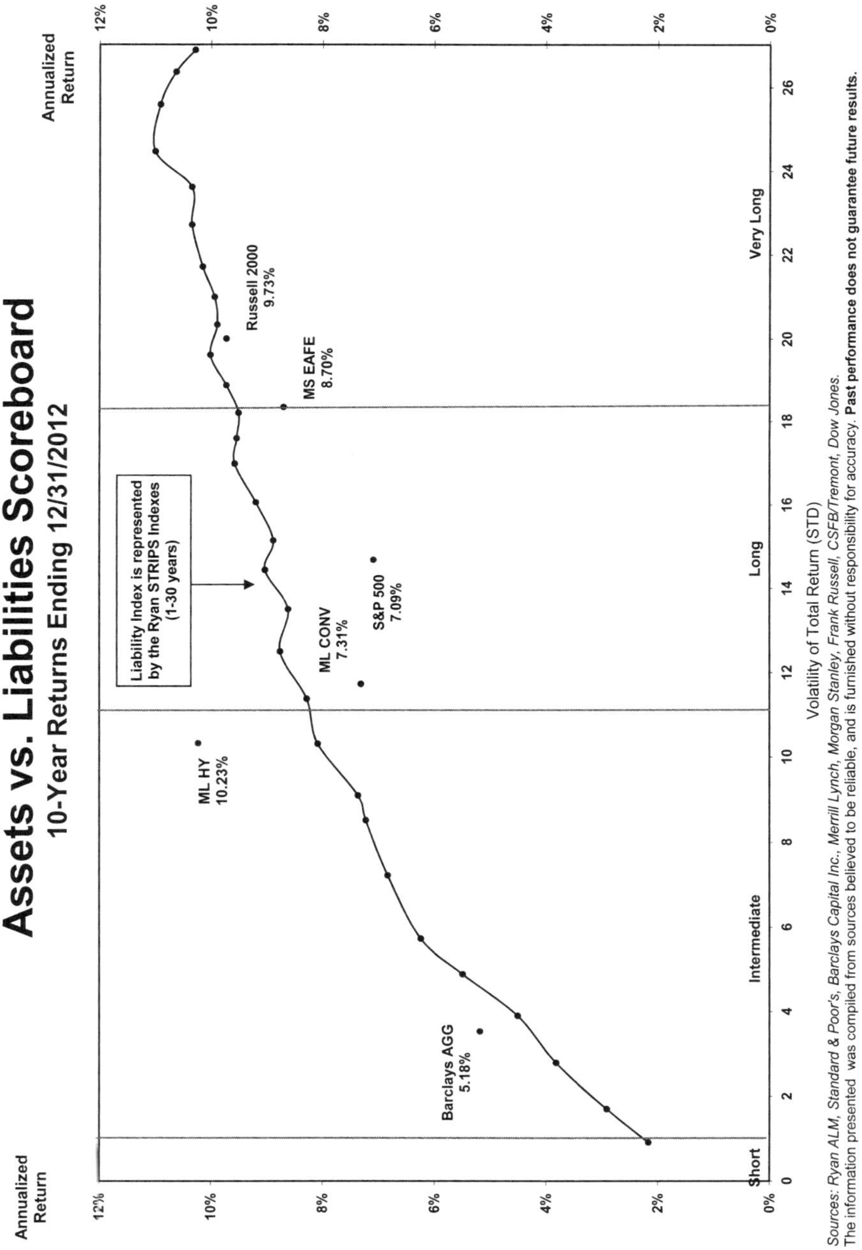

Ryan ALM, Inc.
Assets vs. Liabilities Scoreboard
10-Year Returns Ending 12/31/2012
Annualized Return
12%
10%
8%
6%
4%
2%
0%
Short
Intermediate
Long
Very Long
0
2
4
6
8
10
12
14
16
18
20
22
24
26
Volatility of Total Return (STD)
Liability Index is represented by the Ryan STRIPS Indexes (1-30 years)
Barclays AGG 5.18%
ML HY 10.23%
ML CONV 7.31%
S&P 500 7.09%
MS EAFE 8.70%
Russell 2000 9.73%
Sources: Ryan ALM, Standard & Poor's, Barclays Capital Inc., Merrill Lynch, Morgan Stanley, Frank Russell, CSFB/Tremont, Dow Jones.
The information presented was compiled from sources believed to be reliable, and is furnished without responsibility for accuracy. Past performance does not guarantee future results.

indexes versus the 1-30 year Ryan Treasury STRIPS yield curve indexes with each black circle representing a one-year incremental STRIPS maturity (which equally weighted comprise the Ryan Liability Benchmark Index). As evident in the graph, all non-bond indexes underperformed the Treasury STRIPS Index that had a similar standard deviation (STD). The Lehman/Barclays Aggregate and the Merrill Lynch High Yield indexes were the only indexes that outperformed the Treasury STRIPS index that had a similar STD. It is important to note, as the duration is extended on the liability curve (Treasury STRIPS yield curve), liability returns increased in a rather linear fashion. This demonstrates how interest rate risk dominates the risk/reward of Treasuries and liabilities (systematic risk). This is why it is so critical to match the interest rate risk of liabilities as a term structure. Since most pensions have an average duration of 10 to 15 years, let's examine the black circles on the Treasury STRIPS yield curve between 10 and 15 years. It is obvious that no generic market index outperformed average liabilities. Moreover, there are few generic market indexes that behave like 10- to 15-year Treasury STRIPS, suggesting that asset allocation needs to find more asset classes that behave accordingly.

Pensions need the alpha portfolios to outgrow liability growth as measured by the CLI. Such assets should be *negatively* correlated to interest rates and liabilities to provide the greatest margin of victory especially when interest rates rise. As a result, most bonds do not qualify as alpha asset candidates. The exceptions are high-yield bonds and convertibles. High-yield bonds require enough yield spread cushion so as to potentially earn the annual target liability alpha. Convertible bonds have a play on equities with higher income yields than the dividends of stocks. Apart from bonds, the ocean of financial securities is the oyster bed for alpha. There are so many to choose from as alpha candidates.

The asset allocation model should know and focus on the victory margin versus liabilities that is required for the alpha assets: **annual target liability alpha!** It is based on the funded ratio. Accordingly, the higher the deficit, the higher the annual target liability alpha. This annual target liability alpha should help clarify the types of alpha assets and risk that are needed. A 2% annual target victory should have a less risky profile than a 6% annual target liability alpha (desperately seeking alpha). The duration of the liabilities should also help shape the alpha portfolio(s) selection. A seven-year duration may not allow as much low liquidity assets (i.e., private placements, alternative investments, real estate, timber, etc.) as a 15-year duration time horizon.

Asset/Liability Matching

The core portfolio for any pension fund should be the liability matching portfolio (liability beta portfolio). Its mission should be to *match* and *fund* the liability payments. This requires a custom liability index (CLI) to create and maintain a proper liability beta portfolio. *Dedication*, *immunization* and *interest rate swap* strategies have all been used over the last 30 years to match liabilities. Unfortunately, they each have structural flaws that make them ill-suited to match and fund liabilities.

Dedication

Dedication is the cash flow matching of the future values of assets versus liabilities. This strategy is ideal except that it allows for the use of corporate *coupon* bonds (and even mortgage-backed securities). Such securities have both reinvestment risk and credit risk, given long time horizons. But perhaps more disturbing is that dedication did not match present values. This caused a structural flaw or conflict with the pension accounting rules that measure assets versus liabilities in present values. This present value mismatch led to potential volatile contribution costs since the funded ratio and contributions are calculated annually on the present values of assets versus liabilities. As a result, Wall Street offered **immunization** as the cure.

Immunization

Immunization is the matching of the present value growth (risk/reward behavior) of assets versus liabilities. This process potentially does not match future values. Its structural flaw was that immunization attempted to match the *average* duration of liabilities. Although duration is a proxy for interest rate sensitivity measurement, using the average duration of a term structure does not work mathematically. **You must match each and every liability payment to immunize liabilities, not the average duration.** Stripping long Treasuries is good evidence of this mathematical disparity. The stripped zero-coupon pieces (60 coupon payment STRIPS + 1 principal payment STRIPS) simply do not equal the whole (30-year Treasury) in present values due to two distinct yield curves (STRIPS versus coupon bonds), which creates an arbitrage. Traders strip and reconstitute these Treasury securities on a dynamic daily basis. As a result of this mathematical disparity and a secular trend toward lower rates, immunization lost its luster.

Matching the average duration of liabilities (i.e., immunization methodology) does not mean you have an index or portfolio that matches the interest rate risk of liabilities. You certainly could not defease or immunize interest rate sensitivity for a pension fund with an average 12-year duration by buying a portfolio composed 100% of 12-year duration zero-coupon bonds. To quantify this disparity we ran our Ryan 1-23 year STRIPS indexes in Exhibit 58 (equally weighted = 12-year average duration) versus the Ryan 12-year STRIPS index for the last 10 years (Dec. 31, 2002-Dec. 31, 2012). The results show a monthly tracking deviation of 40 basis points, an annual return difference of -0.88%, and a cumulative return difference of -18.16%. Over a 24-year period (Dec. 31, 1988-Dec. 31, 2012), the tracking deviation was 33 basis points with a **cumulative growth differential of**

EXHIBIT 58

Ryan ALM, Inc
Performance Attribution Report (PAR)

Horizon : 12/31/2002 to 12/31/2012		Ryan Liability 1-23	Ryan Liability 12 (Benchmark)	Difference
RISK				
1. Annualized Standard Deviation	%	11.42	12.50	-1.08
2. Volatility to Benchmark (Beta)		0.90		
3. R-Square	%	97.48		
4. Correlation	%	98.73		
5. STD of Differential Return	bp	63		
6. Tracking Deviation	bp	40		
7. Shortfall Frequency	%	54.17		
8. Average Shortfall	bp	44		
REWARD				
9. Annualized Total Return	%	7.88	8.77	-0.88
10. Cumulative Total Return	%	113.70	131.86	-18.16
11. Excess Return Frequency	%	45.83		
12. Average Excess Return	bp	35		
RISK ADJUSTED RETURNS				
13. Sharpe's Ratio (old)		0.52	0.55	-0.03
14. Information Ratio		-0.40		

All calculations are based on monthly returns

47.98%! You must match or hedge *each* monthly liability benefit payment. If each liability payment is not matched then whenever the yield curve changes shape (which takes about a day), liabilities are no longer matched or hedged. This is why no generic index could ever be a good benchmark for liability growth behavior. Only a custom liability index can value and measure the volatility of the present value of each monthly benefit payment. **Only a custom liability index fund (i.e., a beta portfolio) can match and fund liabilities properly!**

Interest Rate Swap (IRS)

Interest rate swaps have been widely implemented as a hedge for liabilities. But such financial instruments are contracts and not assets. As a result, **you cannot *defease* or *settle* liabilities with interest rate swaps!** If the assets are invested in asset classes that usually have a low correlation to liabilities (i.e., equities) then you certainly cannot match or defease liabilities. In fact, you have a definite mismatch of assets versus liabilities that could be critical, as the decade of 2000 proved. Interest rate swaps in 2000 through 2002 would not have hedged or matched liabilities if the assets were invested in equities and other non-liability matching assets. The volatility of these assets (e.g., equities) remains uncorrelated to liabilities, so the funding ratio is affected accordingly. In the end, interest rate swaps are an asset tool, but not a discount rate or proper liability hedging vehicle.

Interest rate swaps were introduced as the new strategy to match or neutralize the interest rate sensitivity of liabilities. This new strategy allowed pensions to reduce their bond holdings as interest rates were trending lower so they could be more fully invested in equities and other performance vehicles—clearly a factor in the $4 trillion deficit mistake. Instead of reducing risk, interest rate swaps actually increased risk with at least three types of risk associated with these contracts:

First, is *income return risk*. In most IRS contracts, the investor is accepting a fixed rate of income and paying a floating rate (i.e., based on the London Interbank Offered Rate (LIBOR). If interest rates go up over time, then the IRS contract will lose, and the pension plan will have to pay the income difference. Since we have been in a secular trend of lower interest rates since 1982, we now have interest rates at a 40-year low. Given that IRS contracts tend to be long-term (10 to 15 years) it is hard to believe that rates would go down over the life of an IRS contract from today's levels. It is highly probable that IRS contracts will lose in the long term and investors will pay the income difference, which could be sizable. For every 100 basis points that interest rates go above the fixed rate, it costs investors 1% per year (based on a 10-year average duration).

Second, is *price return risk*. The IRS contract supposedly hedges the liability price return by matching the average duration of liabilities. As immunization proved, this is not mathematically accurate. Liabilities are a term structure (yield curve) of benefit payments. We cannot effectively match both the average duration of liabilities as well as each payment of the entire liability term structure. As soon as the shape of the yield curve (discount rates) changes we will get a much different price return behavior. Moreover, an IRS contract is not an asset. Whatever assets are purchased (e.g., equities) must match or exceed the liability price return in order to succeed. This may be a good bet over time, but it is certainly not a hedge or match of liabilities as promoted.

Third, is *counter-party risk*. As the Lehman, Bear Stearns, and MF Global fiascos are such recent and vivid examples, IRS contracts have counter-party risk. It is real and very evident today.

For all the reasons above, IRS contracts should never be the discount rate(s) used to price liabilities or the liability index to measure the risk/reward behavior of liabilities, or the liability beta hedging strategy. They are not a match or perfect hedge of liabilities. They are a tool to better reduce the interest rate sensitivity mismatch of non-bond assets. They never can defease or replace zero-coupon bonds as the matching liability asset portfolio.

Liability *Beta* Portfolio

The mission of the liability beta portfolio is to match and fund liabilities at low risk. This is best accomplished with a portfolio of government zero-coupon bonds matched to the CLI. The liability beta portfolio is actually a liability index fund. Although index funds are quite popular in America, liability index funds are not. Given that the objective of most institutions and individuals is to fund some type of liability schedule, liability index funds should be a core investment. A liability index fund has all the benefits of an index fund, plus valuable features no other index fund can have. The purpose of the liability beta portfolio or liability index fund is to fund each liability payment by matching or replicating the risk/reward of the liability index objective (CLI) at a low tracking error.

Index funds became increasingly attractive due to several factors:

1. **Low tracking error** versus target index benchmark
2. **Lower fees** than most active management fees
3. Consistent **performance** versus index objective
4. **Diversified portfolio**

Since it is difficult to consistently outperform indexes (especially after fees are paid) index funds became an increasingly larger or core investment for many institutional and even retail investors in the last two decades. The largest mutual funds tend to be index funds (e.g., Vanguard). In addition, exchange traded funds (ETFs) have grown significantly to include $1.048 trillion in assets and 1,134 index fund products by the end of 2011,[58] perhaps more so than any other financial product. Also worth noting are the closet index funds, that prefer

58 Investment Company Institute, *2011 Investment Company Fact Book*, 51st ed. http://www.ici.org/pdf/2011_factbook.pdf.

not to be identified with index funds and their lower fees, yet they tend not to stray far from the key characteristics and statistics comprising the index objective (i.e., weightings, sector stratification, yields, modified duration, ratings, etc.). Indeed, it is an index investment world!

The true objective of a pension plan is to fund the liability benefit payment schedule at a stable and low cost to the plan sponsor. With a liability driven objective, only a liability beta portfolio could provide such stability and low cost. The true quest of a pension plan is to be fully funded (or overfunded) and stay there—so that contribution costs are low and stable. In other words, the true quest of the pension allocation is beta, not alpha! Alpha is a temporary or short term goal. Once pensions reach a fully funded status, they want to be beta dominant in their asset allocation so they can reduce contribution costs and the volatility in their funded ratios, which has plagued them since 1999.

The liability beta portfolio is best managed as a liability index fund customized to each pension's unique cash flow schedule. A liability index fund, by definition, requires a custom liability index (CLI) to create or model. Until you match each monthly liability payment (liability term structure), you cannot hedge the interest rate risk (systematic risk) that dominates the risk/reward behavior of liabilities. Unfortunately, the failure of many pension schemes from immunization to interest rate swaps is that they have tried to match only the average duration of liabilities. This is incorrect math. You must match the entire term structure of liabilities (each monthly liability payment) to properly match liabilities. Only through the CLI could you get the present value calculations necessary to understand how to match and monitor the ever-changing shape and risk/reward behavior of a term structure (yield curve) of liabilities.

The old Lehman (now Barclays) Aggregate index, has been the standard index benchmark for most fixed income assets in pensions since the early mid-1980s. Although this index is a good measurement of the bond market, it has little correlation to liabilities. Most pensions have long cash flow structures with volatile risk/reward behaviors much different than the Barclay's Aggregate. To illustrate the disparity between generic traditional bond indexes and liabilities, I compared the Barclays Aggregate to the Ryan Liability Benchmark Index for the last 26 years (ending Dec. 31, 2012). The Ryan Liability Benchmark Index is the Treasury STRIPS yield curve (1-30 years) equally weighted with an average duration of around 15 years while the Barclays Aggregate tends to be around a five-year duration:

EXHIBIT 59

RISK/REWARD COMPARISON (12/31/86 - 12/31/12)

	Barclays Aggregate	Ryan Liability Benchmark
Standard Deviation	3.92	13.02
Correlation	87.12	
Tracking Deviation	214	
Annual Total Return	7.06	9.46
Information Ratio	-0.24	

Ryan Liability Benchmark Index is a proprietary index of Ronald J. Ryan, CFA, and Ryan ALM, Inc. (patent pending)

The Performance Attribution Report (PAR) in Exhibit 60 on the following page provides the data analysis to prove the extreme mismatch of the Barclays Aggregate versus the Ryan Liability Benchmark (which is a better proxy for most pension funds). **However, only a custom liability index weighted by each client's actuarial projections could ever be truly accurate and the best benchmark for asset allocation, asset management, and performance measurement purposes.**

This comparison proves that the most popular bond index benchmark does not behave or correlate well to pension liabilities.

EXHIBIT 60

Ryan ALM, Inc.
Performance Attribution Report (PAR)

Horizon : 12/31/1986 to 12/31/2012		Barclays AGG	Ryan Liability (Benchmark)	Difference
RISK				
1. Annualized Standard Deviation	%	3.92	13.02	-9.10
2. Volatility to Benchmark (Beta)		0.26		
3. R-Square	%	75.90		
4. Correlation	%	87.12		
5. STD of Differential Return	bp	283		
6. Tracking Deviation	bp	214		
7. Shortfall Frequency	%	53.21		
8. Average Shortfall	bp	224		
REWARD				
9. Annualized Total Return	%	7.06	9.46	-2.40
10. Cumulative Total Return	%	489.78	949.74	-459.96
11. Excess Return Frequency	%	46.79		
12. Average Excess Return	bp	202		
RISK ADJUSTED RETURNS				
13. Sharpe's Ratio (old)		0.76	0.41	0.34
14. Information Ratio		-0.24		

All calculations are based on monthly returns.

With a correlation of 87.12, a tracking deviation of 214 bps, and an annual total return difference of -2.40%, the Lehman/Barclays Aggregate has proven to be a huge opportunity cost for the last 26 years for pensions. This data also emphasizes that the market risk in bonds is *interest rate risk*, which dominates the risk/reward behavior of liabilities. Historically, interest rate risk represents over 95% of the total return of investment grade bonds.

No *generic* index should be used as a beta portfolio or benchmark for a liability driven objective! Perhaps the silliest notion of a liability beta portfolio is the S&P 500 or any non-bond index. The S&P 500 as an index fund may be a *market* beta portfolio, but certainly does not correlate or behave like any liability term structure. As the performance attribution report (PAR) in Exhibit 61 clearly shows, the S&P 500 has a negative correlation to liabilities (as measured by the Ryan Liability Benchmark = -29.48%) and has underperformed quite severely from Dec. 31, 1999, to Dec. 31, 2012 (-8.44% annual returns or -225.62% cumulative).

Believe it or not, the S&P 500 has barely outperformed the Treasury STRIPS yield curve (Ryan Liability Benchmark) from Dec. 31, 1986 to Dec. 31, 2012 by just -0.06% annually, equal to 14.34% cumulative for 26 years as shown in Exhibit 62.

A liability beta portfolio can only be a 100% bond portfolio matched to the liability cash flow schedule! You have to create a custom liability index based on the client's actuarial projections of benefit payments to create a beta portfolio that matches the liability objective of pensions (as measured by a CLI).

Portable Alpha

Most portable alpha strategies today not only measure alpha versus a generic market index, but also use the generic market index as their beta portfolio. This is incorrect thinking and inconsistent with any liability objective. Using the S&P 500 (or any generic index) as an index

EXHIBIT 61

Ryan ALM, Inc.
Performance Attribution Report (PAR)

Horizon : 12/31/1999 to 12/31/2012		SP 500	Ryan Liability (Benchmark)	Difference
RISK				
1. Annualized Standard Deviation	%	15.89	13.48	2.41
2. Volatility to Benchmark (Beta)		-0.35		
3. R-Square	%	8.69		
4. Correlation	%	-29.48		
5. STD of Differential Return	bp	686		
6. Tracking Deviation	bp	525		
7. Shortfall Frequency	%	54.49		
8. Average Shortfall	bp	541		
REWARD				
9. Annualized Total Return	%	1.66	10.10	-8.44
10. Cumulative Total Return	%	23.88	249.50	-225.62
11. Excess Return Frequency	%	45.51		
12. Average Excess Return	bp	507		
RISK ADJUSTED RETURNS				
13. Sharpe's Ratio (old)		-0.05	0.57	-0.62
14. Information Ratio		-0.36		

All calculations are based on monthly returns.

EXHIBIT 62

Ryan ALM, Inc.
Performance Attribution Report (PAR)

Horizon : 12/31/1986 to 12/31/2012		SP 500	Ryan Liability (Benchmark)	Difference
RISK				
1. Annualized Standard Deviation	%	15.56	13.02	2.55
2. Volatility to Benchmark (Beta)		-0.06		
3. R-Square	%	0.22		
4. Correlation	%	-4.65		
5. STD of Differential Return	bp	600		
6. Tracking Deviation	bp	437		
7. Shortfall Frequency	%	47.12		
8. Average Shortfall	bp	459		
REWARD				
9. Annualized Total Return	%	9.51	9.46	0.06
10. Cumulative Total Return	%	964.08	949.74	14.34
11. Excess Return Frequency	%	52.88		
12. Average Excess Return	bp	416		
RISK ADJUSTED RETURNS				
13. Sharpe's Ratio (old)		0.35	0.41	-0.06
14. Information Ratio		0.00		

All calculations are based on monthly returns.

fund could *never* represent the liability beta portfolio or have the risk/reward behavior of the cash flow of a client's liability schedule. That is also true for every asset class except zero-coupon bonds matched to liabilities. Using inappropriate asset classes and generic portable alpha strategies, a pension fund could lose in at least three ways:

1. **Alpha portfolio loses to liabilities (CLI)**

2. **Beta portfolio loses to liabilities (does not match liabilities)**

3. **Performance fee paid on wrong alpha measurement**

The asset side must be in sync with the liability objective if the asset side is to function in harmony with the pension objective. Without a CLI, how can asset allocation, asset management and performance measurement work properly? They all link to the liability objective as best measured by the funded ratio (assets/liabilities in market value dollars). There needs to be coordination and orchestration of all asset functions in harmony with **the true objective: funding liabilities at low and stable cost, with reduced risk to the plan sponsor.**

Liability Beta Portfolio as Risk-Free Assets

Years ago, I had the unique pleasure of brainstorming with the Nobel Prize winner Bill Sharpe. He is certainly one of the most outstanding intellects I have ever encountered. He was also a good listener. I explained to him how I thought that the risk-free asset was always the asset that matched the objective with certainty, rather than the Sharpe ratio approach, which uses the lowest volatility asset as the risk-free asset (e.g., three-month T-Bill). I gave Prof. Sharpe two examples to prove my point:

1. Objective = S&P 500

The lowest risk asset with this objective would be an S&P 500 index fund or exchange traded fund (ETF) that matches the objective with certainty. The three-month T-Bill would be a very risky asset as it could never match with any certainty the risk/reward behavior of the S&P 500. Prof. Sharpe agreed.

2. Objective = Liabilities

Liabilities tend to be a schedule of monthly payments extending far out into the future, so I asked Prof. Sharpe what is the lowest risk asset I could buy to fund the 10-year liability. His reply was that a 10-year Treasury zero-coupon bond that matches the liability payment with *certainty* would be the *risk-free* asset with that objective. Prof. Sharpe asserted that the three-month T-Bill would be very risky since it would have 39 reinvestment moments, that is, 39 moments of uncertainty over a 10-year horizon.

I concluded with the obvious fact that **the objective decides what the risk-free asset is.** We cannot have a *generic* risk-free asset that applies to all objectives—especially liability objectives—since each pension is a unique set of cash flows with its own liability benefit payment schedule. Therefore, I asserted that the best definition of risk is:

Risk is best defined as the uncertainty of meeting the client objective! The greater the uncertainty, the greater the risk.

Accordingly, **if the liability objective is best measured as a custom liability index, then a custom liability index fund is the risk-free asset!** Bill Sharpe agreed and proceeded to create a new Sharpe ratio that focuses on the objective and not the three-month T-Bill.

The industry uses this concept as the *information ratio*. Thank you, Prof. Sharpe, for your diligence and responsiveness.

Pension and Investment Performance Evaluation Report (PIPER) Study

The PIPER is the oldest and most comprehensive performance study of asset management available today. In fixed income it consistently shows that there is little or no value added in *active* bond management. For almost any time horizon, the PIPER study shows that the **median** bond manager underperforms or barely outperforms the popular bond market benchmark, the Lehman/Barclays Aggregate Index (see Exhibit 63). However, this study is based on performance value calculated *before fees are added.* After fees (at 30 bps) are factored into the equation, the median bond manager consistently underperforms the bond market (as measured by the Lehman/Barclays Aggregate Index).

EXHIBIT 63

PERFORMANCE OF DOMESTIC FIXED INCOME MANAGERS (INVESTMENT GRADE)

Last 10 yrs ending:	12/31/08	12/31/09	12/31/10
1st Quartile	5.75%	6.92%	6.87%
Median	5.22%	6.46%	6.12
Barclays Aggregate	5.63%	6.33%	5.80

Source: *Pensions & Investments*, (as calculated by Morningstar)

Logically, if 50% of an asset class consistently underperforms its market benchmark, one should index that asset class! As a result, bonds are best managed *passively* as index funds. It then follows that pensions need to reconsider the use of investment grade bonds.

Investment grade bonds should be the core portfolio (liability beta portfolio) but ***not*** be actively managed versus *generic* bond market indexes. Instead, investment grade bonds should be managed *passively* as the liability matching portfolio. This rearrangement of investment grade bonds from active to passive management will also save fees and eliminate tracking deviations versus liabilities. The real question is which index to use? The obvious answer is **the index that best represents the client objective**. If the objective is liability driven, only a custom liability index could best represent the true client objective. As a result, bonds should be managed as liability index funds (i.e., the liability beta, or core portfolio). The benefits of a liability index fund (liability beta portfolio) are numerous:

1. Reduces Volatility in Funded Ratio

If you match liabilities, then you match the risk/reward behavior of the present value of liabilities. This eliminates the roller coaster effect that most plans have in their funded ratio due to a mismatching of assets vs. liabilities. This erratic growth difference between assets versus liabilities plays havoc with budgets (i.e., contributions), benefit decisions, and financial statements.

2. Reduces Volatility in Contribution Cost

If you match liabilities, then the funded ratio is less volatile, which in turns means that contribution costs become less volatile. Utopia is to match and ***fully fund*** liabilities consistently, so that few or no contributions are ever needed.

3. Reduces Interest Rate Risk

As the FASB rules (and common sense) suggest, liabilities behave like a high-quality zero-coupon bond portfolio. As a result, liabilities are highly duration and interest rate sensitive. A liability beta portfolio or liability index fund matches the interest rate sensitivity of liabilities and neutralizes this risk factor.

4. Reduces Bond Asset Management Fees

A liability index fund should save clients significantly on their bond asset management fees.

5. Monitors True Economic Behavior of Liabilities

A custom liability index is the proper benchmark for liability driven objectives. It creates a true market value measurement of liabilities instead of the hypothetical rates (GASB, PPA MAP-21) or single discount rate approach (GASB) used by most pensions today. Unlike actuarial reports that come out annually, or even triennially and months delinquent, a custom liability index needs to be frequent and accurate. Imagine if the S&P 500 came out annually, months delinquent. Who would use it as a benchmark?

6. Proper Benchmark for Assets

Assets need a proper liability benchmark to understand and monitor the true relative performance of assets versus liabilities. As a result, a true economic funded ratio can be ascertained frequently, which supports asset allocation decisions, asset management decisions, benefit decisions, contribution decisions, and performance measurement evaluations—they all link to an accurate and frequent economic funded ratio. Performance measurement can now accurately measure the growth of assets versus the growth of liabilities to assess true economic alpha.

7. Creates Lowest Cost/Lowest Risk Portfolio

(Liability Beta Portfolio)

The liability index fund is the proper liability beta portfolio that matches the true liability objective. Such a portfolio of government zeroes is the lowest cost/lowest risk portfolio for the pension plan. It reduces interest rate risk and the volatility of the funded ratio, as well as lowers contribution costs, as matched liabilities require no extra contributions.

8. Core Portfolio (Matches Assets vs. Liabilities)

The liability index fund should be the liability beta portfolio or core portfolio. **The true quest of any pension or liability driven objective is to reach and maintain a fully funded liability matched asset position, such that contribution costs remain low and stable over the future (true pension objective).** This can be best achieved with a zero-coupon bond portfolio that matches chronologically and fully funds the unique cash flow liability of any pension plan. Any other asset class does not match the behavior of liabilities and creates the roller coaster effect of victories (surplus) and defeats (deficits).

"An error is not a mistake until you refuse to correct it."

—John F. Kennedy

CHAPTER **SIXTEEN**

PENSION SOLUTION: PERFORMANCE ATTRIBUTION

Performance measurement and attribution is the last gear in the asset/liability system. It measures and monitors the risk/reward behavior of assets versus their objective. Asset managers are hired and fired based on their *relative* performance versus an index objective. Traditionally, assets are given a generic market index as their objective. As I have emphasized several times in this book, until pension assets are measured versus the liability objective, it is difficult for the pension plan trustees and their consultant to understand if assets are performing well, or better yet—if asset allocation performed well.

The reason why liabilities are "missing in action" in performance measurement is because there is no liability index with which to compare the assets. This absence of a liability benchmark can be explained in large part by the fact that pension liabilities are traditionally calculated annually and reported months after the fact! Moreover, the liability benefit payment schedule is usually not provided as part of the actuarial annual report. More importantly, the calculation or present value pricing of liabilities is very confusing; it's caught up in a jabberwocky of accounting rules and actuarial practices such that the asset side is unclear as to the present value calculation of liabilities on a current basis. It is extremely difficult, if not impossible, for an asset manager to manage against an invisible opponent such as liabilities. It is just as difficult to monitor assets versus liabilities without a custom liability index. Imagine playing sports without a scoreboard, or worse, getting the wrong score. A successful sports team adjusts their strategy depending on whether they are way ahead or way behind, as well as how much time is left. Just like in sports, the pension game needs a scoreboard to alert all players to the relative score of assets versus liabilities. The asset allocation strategy should be adjusted over time depending on whether the funded ratio is way ahead (surplus), or way behind (deficit).

Until a custom liability index is installed, performance measurement and attribution will never know if asset allocation and asset management are doing their proper job of enhancing the funded ratio. The first performance test should be to **analyze the performance of asset allocation**. This is seldom done. Since asset allocation is the key decision, it should be analyzed and monitored just like any asset manager. Total asset growth behavior should be compared against total liability risk/reward behavior as shown in Exhibit 64. In this exhibit, total assets underperformed total liabilities by 8.72% annually, and 27.00% cumulatively over three years, thereby eroding the funded ratio and creating more contribution costs. Moreover, asset allocation was a failure since its job was to outgrow liabilities by enough each year to reach full funding over a certain time horizon (i.e., duration of liabilities). Assuming a 30% deficit (funded ratio = 70%) and a duration of 12 years suggests that asset allocation needs to outgrow liabilities by 3.57% per year ([30%/12 years] / 70%) to reach a fully funded status in 12 years. Since asset allocation produced a -8.72% additional deficit per year versus liabilities, it was a dismal failure and cost the pension additional contribution costs.

Graphing assets versus liabilities as a yield curve scatter diagram (see Exhibit 65, page 166) is also useful in showing the relative risk/

EXHIBIT 64

Ryan ALM, Inc.
Performance Attribution Report (PAR)

Horizon : 12/31/2007 to 12/31/2010		Total Assets	Ryan Liability (Benchmark)	Difference
RISK				
1. Annualized Standard Deviation	%	21.83	17.76	4.07
2. Volatility to Benchmark (Beta)		-0.22		
3. R-Square	%	3.20		
4. Correlation	%	-17.90		
5. STD of Differential Return	bp	893		
6. Tracking Deviation	bp	719		
7. Shortfall Frequency	%	47.22		
8. Average Shortfall	bp	829		
REWARD				
9. Annualized Total Return	%	-2.84	5.88	-8.72
10. Cumulative Total Return	%	-8.29	18.71	-27.00
11. Excess Return Frequency	%	52.78		
12. Average Excess Return	bp	620		
RISK ADJUSTED RETURNS				
13. Sharpe's Ratio (old)		-0.18	0.27	-0.45
14. Information Ratio		-0.29 All		

calculations are based on monthly returns.

EXHIBIT 65

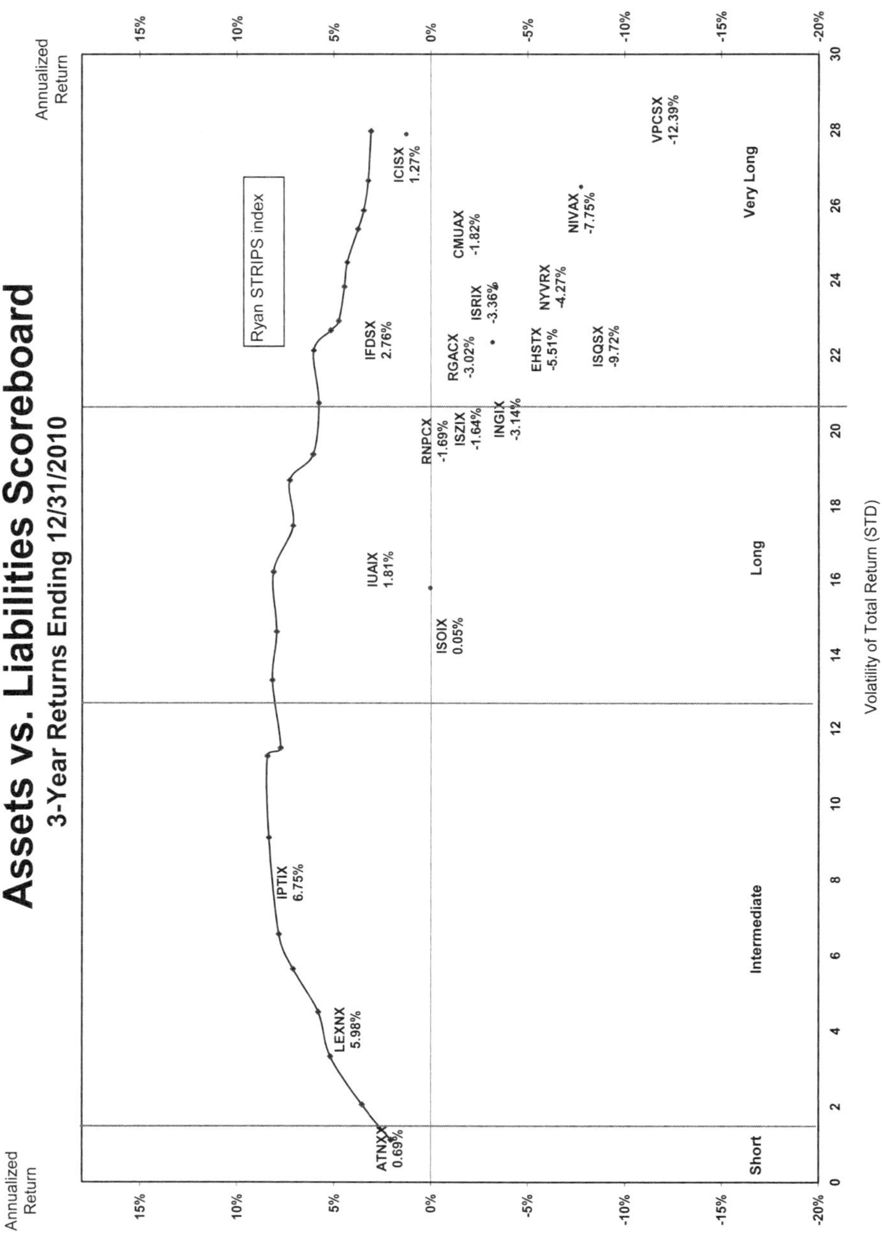
Ryan ALM, Inc.
Assets vs. Liabilities Scoreboard
3-Year Returns Ending 12/31/2010
Annualized Return
Volatility of Total Return (STD)
Ryan STRIPS index
Short
Intermediate
Long
Very Long
ATNX 0.69%
LEXNX 5.98%
IPTIX 6.75%
IUAIX 1.81%
ISOIX 0.05%
RNPCX -1.69%
ISZIX -1.64%
INGIX -3.14%
IFDSX 2.76%
RGACX -3.02%
ISRIX -3.36%
CMUAX -1.82%
EHSTX -5.51%
NYVRX -4.27%
ISQSX -9.72%
NIVAX -7.75%
ICISX 1.27%
VPCSX -12.39%

reward behavior of each asset manager (and total assets) versus liabilities. In this three-year graph, liabilities are represented by a black line with dots for each annual maturity STRIPS. Each asset manager is cited by a name symbol with annualized return. It is clear that all managers but two underperformed the liability line, suggesting that the asset team did not add value or earn liability alpha over three years. As a result, asset allocation did not perform yet.

The next step is the performance attribution of **each asset manager versus liabilities**. Each asset manager should be measured versus the liabilities it is funding as shown in Exhibit 64, or as in the graph in Exhibit 65, to see its relative risk/reward behavior versus liabilities. In the final analysis, there should never be an asset review meeting without a review of liabilities as well. Included should be a review of the funded ratio, the asset allocation, and the asset management versus the liability objective. Pension plan sponsors need to stay focused on their stated objective of funding liabilities at low cost by requiring that all asset decisions be in harmony with this objective, such that contribution costs are low and stable. This quest requires accurate and frequent monitoring of assets versus liabilities as measured by a custom liability index.

"Without a pension scoreboard, you can't play the pension game!"

—Ronald J. Ryan, CFA

CHAPTER **SEVENTEEN**

CONCLUSION

The pension crisis is the largest financial dilemma this country has faced since the Great Depression. The pension deficits of private and public plans are estimated to exceed $4 trillion as of the end of 2012. If TARP I was a national emergency at $800 billion—what do we call this? More importantly, we must acknowledge the true cause of this pension crisis: inappropriate accounting rules that mispriced pension assets and liabilities, causing exaggerated funded ratios which led to inappropriate asset allocation, benefit, and contribution decisions...it all links! From 1999 on, smoothing of assets tended to *overvalue* pension assets, and GASB's use of the ROA as the discount rate to value liabilities counterproductively *undervalued* liabilities by 24% to 70%. FASB's allowance of using the ROA instead of actual asset returns lowered pension expense and even raised EPS artificially (phantom earnings). However, such inappropriate accounting rules eventually created an actuarial loss amortization that will haunt and hurt future EPS of most companies for several years to come.

The solution to the pension crisis starts with the financial truth: economic books. The establishment of economic books comes in the form of a custom liability index (CLI). The CLI prices liabilities at market value (Treasury STRIPS) as well as in compliance to ASC 715(FAS No.158), PPA (three segment and spot rates), and GASB (ROA). The CLI displays and compares each discount rate method versus the true market valuation (economic books) so pensions can understand their true economic funded ratio. Asset allocation should then be focused and based on this economic funded ratio, such that a large deficit has a radically different and more aggressive asset allocation than a surplus position (where asset allocation would be very conservative). Had this been the procedure in the decade of the 1990s, the $4 trillion pension deficit would not have accumulated. Unfortunately, pension plan sponsors focused instead on achieving an ROA hurdle rate, which misled them and misdirected asset decisions.

Asset management should be segregated into two distinct categories:

1. **Liability alpha** assets have a mission to outgrow liabilities as measured by the custom liability index (CLI). Alpha is measured as the excess growth (return) vs. the CLI growth rate.

2. **Liability beta** assets have a mission to match and fund liabilities. Such a beta portfolio is best structured as a liability index fund. This requires a CLI to construct and maintain such a liability beta portfolio. The liability beta portfolio should be the *core* portfolio of any pension. Pension plan sponsors should reconsider *active* bond management and replace it with *passive* bond management in the form of a liability beta portfolio.

As the funded ratio improves, there should be regular corrections to the asset allocation, whereby more is allocated to the beta assets to secure the "victory" and reduce the volatility of the funded ratio and contribution costs. While the industry refers to this as dynamic or tactical asset allocation, I call it ***responsive* asset allocation**. Performance measurement should monitor total assets versus total liabilities (as measured by the CLI) to ensure that the asset allocation is achieving the intended goal of a fully funded plan. This enhanced pension asset/liability management (ALM) system is now focused and in harmony with the true pension objective: **to fund liabilities in such a way that contribution costs remain low and stable over the future!**

Previously, liabilities were "missing in action" in every critical asset decision and asset review. It was difficult to find liabilities in the asset allocation, asset management, and performance measurement decisions and reports. With the installation of a custom liability index, all of the asset decisions can fit together like a mosaic and be in harmony with the true client liability objective. The board of trustees can effectively make well-informed decisions on asset allocation, benefits, and contributions because they are now being provided with accurate and frequent calculations of the economic funded ratio, including liability growth and liability present values. Pension consultants can now recommend proper asset allocation action in response to this economic funded ratio calculation. Moreover, consultants will be able to accurately assess the performance measurement of asset managers versus liabilities, as well as the success of the asset allocation process. **Indeed, with the installation of a custom liability index, the missing piece has been found that connects all asset decisions to the true pension objective of reaching and maintaining a fully funded plan, such that contribution costs remain low and stable over the life of the plan.**

***"When you come to the end of your rope,
tie a knot and hang on."***

—Franklin D Roosevelt

TESTIMONY OF RONALD J. RYAN BEFORE ERISA ADVISORY COUNCIL

UNITED STATES DEPARTMENT OF LABOR

Employee Retirement Income Security Act

Advisory Council on Employee Welfare and Pension Benefit Plans

★ ★ ★

The Working Group on Defined Benefit Funding

★ ★ ★

Thursday
July 24, 2003

The group met at 9:00 a.m. in Conference Suite N 3437 B C of the Frances Perkins Building, 200 Constitution Avenue, N.W., Washington, D.C. at 9:00 a.m. Dana Muir, Chair, presiding.

PRESENT:

Dana Muir	Chair
Mark Bongard	Member
Todd Gardenhire	Member
John S. Miller	Member
Thomas Nyhan	Member
Antoinette Pilzner	Member
Norman Stein	Member
John Szczur	Member
Ronnie Sue Thierman	Member
Donald B. Trone	Member
David Wray	Member
Sharon Morrissey	Executive Secretary

CHAIRPERSON MUIR: Our next witness is Ron Ryan, from Ryan Labs. And Ronald J. Ryan is the founder and the President of Ryan Labs, which manages over three billion dollars in assets.

Previously, Mr. Ryan headed the Ryan Financial Strategy Group, which created the first daily bond index in the United States, the Treasury yield curve, which is syndicated throughout the world.

Mr. Ryan built Ryan Labs as an asset management and research firm, specializing in custom index funds since 1988. He's well-known for his innovative work on fixed income indexes and research, especially asset/liability management.

I was told at break that he is the grandfather of the Lehman indices. I'm sure they just mean he's the father of the Lehman indices.

(Laughter.)

CHAIRPERSON MUIR: But Mr. Ryan has worked with bonds since at least 1966, as I went back through his work in bond and in indices since 1973. He holds the Chartered Financial Analyst designation.

He has both an MBA and a BBA from Loyola University. And, he's up.

MR. RYAN: I am honored to present my views on retirement DB funding and discount rate issues, with possible solutions. We believe there is a pension crisis in America that threatens the solvency and financial integrity of our corporations, our cities, our states and even the federal government.

The size of the pension underfunding suggests that this is the largest financial dilemma since the S&L crisis of the 1980s. Corporations have to fill out IRS Form 5500, if their pension plan is underfunded by greater than $50 million.

At the end of 2002, the deficit recorded here was close to $250 billion. According to the Wilshire annual report on state retirement systems pensions, the public state fund deficit was another $94 billion.

In both cases, the discount rates used to calculate such deficits were higher than market rates, suggesting these deficits are much larger than presented. And, according to the CATO Institute, our Social Security liability totals over $20 trillion, the largest liability in the world, with about $5 trillion in assets that are subject to Congressional withdrawals for operating budget needs.

Since your focus here is on corporate pension plans, we will address this area only. The pension crisis I envision shows up as four problems for corporate financial statements. Please see page 8.

First is earnings drag. Second is higher contributions. Third is higher variable PBGC premiums. And fourth is lower funding status. In an effort to educate, as well as monitor, the pension asset liability status of our clients, I created the first liability index in America in 1991. Please see page 9.

It was trademarked in 1992. This index consists of 100% Treasury zero-coupon bonds, equally weighted, with an average duration of 15.5 years. Such an index conforms to FAS 87, and is a good proxy for the average pension plan liability growth behavior.

In practice, we customize this index to match each client's actuarial benefits schedule and produce accurate measurements of pension liability size, structure, and growth.

On page 10, using a static asset allocation of 5% cash, 30% bonds, 60% domestic equities, 5% international equities, which tends to be the pension industry standard, based upon many P&I surveys.

Pension assets have, on average, underperformed pension liabilities by -67.83% over the last three calendar years. Page 11 shows that if a pension DB plan was fully funded on December 1988, it would be 57% funded at the end of 2002.

The reason for such skewness to equities lies within accounting and actuarial rules of practices that mislead pension funds into inappropriate asset allocation decisions.

The true villain of the pension crisis is the pension pencil. If you think the Enron pencil was interesting, wait until you see the pension pencil. Please meet "Woody".

Woody can enhance your earnings; it can reduce your liabilities any time you want. The ROA is on page 12. Corporations are earnings-led, ROA-led, they're not liability-led.

Since pensions are an expense on the income statement, corporations want this cost minimized, if not removed. The offset to this pension cost is the return on pension assets, ROA.

Accounting practices allow for corporations to forecast the ROA a year in advance. If you know your pension expenses a year in advance, you know the ROA needed to wash out those costs.

But why stop there? If you raise the ROA above the break-even needed to wash out pension expense, you will create pension income that enhances earnings. Thank you, Woody.

Indeed, this procedure has become a national trend, such that about 10% of earnings per share for companies in the S&P are attributable to pension income. Pension accounting rules (FASB) allow this optimistic forecast of ROA if the auditors can validate the ROA from historical return behaviors.

All asset classes are treated this way, except bonds, where the current yield to maturity is used, and not historical return patterns. This has led to a reduction in bond allocations as interest rates kept going down for several years, and an increase in equities, as well as hedge funds and alternative investments, which either have historical returns that validate the ROA or have returns that are not market returns, but book value or appraised value-based (hypothetical).

For example, private equity and real estate. As a result, bonds are the low-risk asset, are the matching liability asset, have not been promoted for asset allocation as its market yield has fallen below the ROA forecast for the last 10 years.

The ROA forecast has been rather constant, averaging 9.2% for the S&P. The difference between the forecasted ROA and actual returns for each year are amortized, usually, over the average life of the pension plan, which is about 10 to 15 years.

This amortization is called actuarial gain and loss. The exhibit on page 13 shows that the last three calendar years had a mismatch of ROA versus the actual returns of about 47% cumulative, resulting in an amortization of about -3% of pension assets, as an actuarial loss annually for the next 12-14 years.

Corporations don't want earnings volatility. So this smoothing process was invented as a compromise to FAS 87. However, it has now taken a short-term problem and made it a recurring long-term earnings drag, which most security analysts will discount more heavily.

Warren Buffett has warned corporations that too high an ROA risks litigation for the CFO, the Board, and the auditors. Naturally, corporations don't want to reduce the ROA, since it would damage earnings immediately for that year with more amortization.

The exhibit on page 14 shows the earnings cost of just a 1% reduction in the ROA for several large corporations is huge. The liability side of the equation has a similar situation.

FAS 87 requires the discounting of liabilities, as a high quality bond yield curve and annuity rates. Page 15 quotes FAS 87, paragraph 199 and paragraph 44, which are clear that you are to use individual discount rates—a yield curve.

They even give an example where the one-year T-bill, the seven-year note and the 30-year bond are all cited as having different interest rates. Page 16 quotes the SEC who, since 1993, has warned corporations to follow the FASB guidelines or face financial restatements and civil or criminal penalties.

The SEC believes the guidance provided by FAS 106, paragraph 186, for medical liabilities, applies to pensions as well. Page 17 quotes FAS 106, paragraph 186, which is quite clear that you are to price liabilities as a high quality zero-coupon bond portfolic, whose par values match the liability payment amount, and whose maturities match the liability payment dates.

Liabilities are a bond portfolio, a high quality zero-coupon bond portfolio. Most DB plans want to price liabilities at the highest discount rate that they can qualify under FAS 87, to reduce the size of their liabilities, which will lower pension expense.

Typically, the Moody's Aa corporate rate is chosen. This index was invented in 1929, and represents only long corporates, not a yield curve. Our critique of this index is attached in the appendix section that you have as a separate handout.

Page 18 explains that actuaries use a discount rate as a forecast of long-term growth for liabilities. For example, the return on liabilities, ROL, as the complement of the ROA for assets.

This forecast is then compared to the actual growth of liabilities for the fiscal year. And the difference is then amortized over the average life of the pension, around 10 to 15 years.

Companies don't want volatility in their financials, so the amortization is supposed to smooth out such volatility. However, actuaries never use market yield curve rates as discount rates.

Instead, they use a single rate to price all liabilities, which is usually 1% or higher in yield. Page 19 calculates how this inaccuracy leads to an amortization on the liability side, that can be quite large, as the Moody's rate, the expected ROL, was 26% too low in estimated growth for the last three years, causing a 1.74% amortization of pension liabilities for the next 12 years.

When the asset and liability side amortizations are added together, to equal a total actuarial gain loss, we find out the total earnings drag. Our exhibit on page 20 tries to isolate this actuarial gain loss dilemma, facing most corporations with a DB plan.

If earnings are $1 billion, with pension assets at $7 billion and pension liabilities at $10 billion, for a 30% deficit, the last three calendar years asset allocation and discount rate pricing, or mis-pricing, would cause a $393 million earnings drag each year for the next 12 years, equal to a 39.3% reduction of last year's earnings of $1 billion.

Indeed, General Motors reported a 33% decline in 2002 earnings per share from this amortization. S&P has forecasted the average earnings drag for the S&P 500 will be around negative 15% for the next few years.

Since the S&P does not have historical earnings growth of 15% per year, it seems that we will have a low or no earnings growth for the S&P for the foreseeable future.

Corporations don't want added costs. Pension contributions are an additional cost that is paid annually, and quite often not budgeted. Corporations want a pension holiday, no pension contribution.

Since the contribution is based on the asset/liability funding ratio, the IRS rules 404(a) and 412(l) apply. As the exhibit on page 21 shows, the IRS uses a weighted average formula discount rate, based on the last four years of the 30-year Treasury, with a corridor of 90-120% of that weighted rate.

Such a formula would never represent the current market yield. Based on this formula, as of June 30, 2003, this weighted discount rate would be 4.81%, versus the 5.30% average for 2002.

It would take a yield of 5.56%, at year-end 2003, to match last year's average discount rate. Page 22, most, if not all, of the FASB and IRS interpretations are done to enhance financial statements, with little concern for the asset side.

Imagine that you are asked to manage the assets of a DB plan. You're told the objective is to fund the pension liabilities at the lowest cost and lowest risk to the plan. You're then given liabilities in the following manner:

First, priced as a single discount rate. Second, it's not a market rate. Third, it's calculated annual, several months delinquent. And fourth, the liability portfolio's not provided.

Could you manage assets, or perform the asset allocation decisions, with this information? Could you function versus the S&P 500, or any asset index, if it came out annually, months delinquent, and you never saw the portfolio and the prices used were not market prices?

Of course not… so, how could the liability side operate any differently? The solutions are obvious, page 23. Until liabilities are priced at the market, with complete transparency and accuracy, we run the risk of an asset/liability disconnect, similar to the S&L crisis.

Liability should be priced at the market as a yield curve. A rule should be created, or enforced, that reads: If you cannot buy it, you cannot use it as a discount rate!

The Moody's Aa rate is not purchasable as a yield curve. Corporate zero-coupon bonds don't exist, they're not purchasable. The Salomon pension yield curve index is not purchasable. Corporate coupon bonds are not purchasable past 15-year duration. You can't buy the Lehman Aggregate since most of the bonds don't have enough liquidity. Can you imagine the fees in pension liabilities with Aa corporate bonds and, as Jeremy Gold said, just one issuer defaults over the 30 years.

Bond indexes are market weighted; they're not liability weighted. They include bonds with options, namely call features, which distort or don't match the liability payment date.

The solution starts with the Treasury zero-coupon yield curve—STRIPS. At the moment, these are the only zeroes that can be purchased in size for every maturity of the Treasury yield curve.

The fact remains; there are no corporate zero-coupon bonds. Until a custom liability index is built for each pension plan, based upon the unique actuarial term structure shape of that plan, and priced off real zero-coupon bonds, pension assets are in jeopardy of managing versus the wrong objective(s).

Currently, pension assets are managed versus generic asset market indices, not liability indices. If you outperform the S&P 500, but lose to liabilities: You lose. We should demand accurate accounting of pension assets and liabilities.

Only marked to market accounting provides this. Pension asset/liability management should not come in the form of incorrect pricing that affects the asset/liability balance. You never hear of state lotteries having an asset/liability problem, and yet they are required by law to invest 100% in government securities, usually, only Treasury zeroes.

We should demand pricing of pension liabilities off the Treasury zero yield curve, weighted by the actuarial benefit schedule. Once a custom liability index is in place, the assets side can function.

Asset allocation and performance measurement models can now compare, accurately, the growth and risk behavior of assets versus liabilities, by term structure. The exhibit on Page 24 demonstrates the need and benefits of a liability index.

The graph depicts the 10-year risk/reward behavior of several key asset classes, shown as dots versus the liability timeline, which is the Treasury zero-coupon yield curve—STRIPS.

Notice that the S&P 500 on the right had an annual return of 9.34%. Notice that the Lehman Aggregate on the left had an annual return of 7.51%. First impressions would suggest that the S&P 500 outperformed the Lehman Aggregate, or bonds, by 1.83% each year.

However, prudent asset allocation would suggest that you use short assets to fund short liabilities, and long assets to fund long liabilities. On closer inspection, the S&P 500 is below the liability line while the Lehman Aggregate is above the line suggesting the Lehman Aggregate won and the S&P 500 lost to liability growth.

The S&P 500 lost to long liabilities by 2.67% per year over the last 10 years. Believe it or not, the 20-year Treasury zero-coupon bond outperformed the S&P 500 by 2.67% annually for the 10 years ending December, 2002.

If asset classes are not measured versus liabilities, then assets seemingly have the wrong index objective. In the words of Confucius, given the wrong index objective you will get the wrong risk/reward behavior.

America has the wrong indexes as their objective. Only a liability index, customized to a pension plan's actuarial schedule, could ever properly calculate and measure each pension's true asset liability position.

Similar to a doctor-patient relationship, you cannot help the pension patient until you run accurate tests, accurate pricing of the liabilities to see what and where the problem is.

If the tests are flawed with inaccurate data, the doctor may prescribe the wrong pricing medicine, or want to perform improper asset allocation surgery. Since pension assets and pension liabilities are the largest assets and liabilities of America, it behooves us to act correctly, even if it causes some pain.

A band-aid or accounting cover-up medication will not cure the pension crisis. Don't help the pension crisis by mispricing liabilities. Price liabilities accurately, off a purchasable Treasury zero-coupon yield curve.

Provide pension relief by relaxing contributions until there is a significant asset/liability deficit. God bless America, God bless America's pensions. Thank you.

CHAIRPERSON MUIR: The floor is open.

MEMBER BONGARD: What kind of transition would you recommend, assuming Congress went in this direction?

MR. RYAN: If contributions were not allowed to be made until the deficit was, say, 30% or greater? And then over the course of years, you raised the level. So, initially it's 70% funding, and then it goes to 75% and then 80%, 85%, 90%.

Give them time to heal their wounds, but let them know you're watching this correctly.

MEMBER BONGARD: Would that be a 10-year period, seven-year period?

MR. RYAN: That's a good question. They most probably need five to 10 years.

MEMBER BONGARD: What do you think most employers would do that sponsor these plans, if such a fix were enacted?

MR. RYAN: Well, the initial reaction is negative, but it's like anything in life, most people don't want to take the medicine because it tastes bad or it hurts. But when you start getting relief, and you heal, I think you appreciate it.

MEMBER MILLER: You had an earnings—your earnings drag chart. What was the earnings enhancement of the pension plan system, prior to the downturn of the markets? Was it 10%, or—

MR. RYAN: According to the S&P, it's in the neighborhood of 12%.

MEMBER MILLER: Twelve percent, okay.

MEMBER GARDENHIRE: In the morning session, we had witness after witness promote the long-term high-grade corporate bond as an alternative index to the 30-year.

MR. RYAN: Yes.

MEMBER GARDENHIRE: And the underlying message seemed to be the whole time, is that this can't be solved it's going to go on, and all that. And what you, and the guy in front of you, said if I listened and heard what you all said, you all have been more concerned with the protection of the participants, by not going to that long-term corporate bond, but by going to a Treasury-based—both of you seem to say that Treasury-based yield curves as a way to protect participants.

Then, and these are my words not your words, bail out the companies that have, for some reason, gotten into problems. Is that a fair interpretation of what I'm hearing?

MR. RYAN: Yes, you know, it's hard to solve the problem if you don't know what it is. I'm sure you would love to go to your ATM machine and it says that you have a $3 million checking account balance when you know you don't.

We need to know the truth. I can't cure a problem if I don't know what it is. Now, AA corporates the pension plan would love it because it's a higher discount rate, right?

But it's artificial, hypothetical. Wall Street would love it, because in order for you to match or beat that rate, you know what you're going to have to buy? Single A and Baa bonds.

Guess where the best profits are on Wall Street? They're not with the Treasury securities, where they make a 64/128th. It's with A's and Baa's, where it works in integers. They could make huge profits.

And, they're not very liquid. We don't have a bond exchange. We don't know the price of most securities, except Treasuries that come across real-time on the broker screens and the Bloomberg's.

A wonderful way to make money, when people don't know right from wrong, good price from bad price.

MEMBER GARDENHIRE: You've got the Chamber of Commerce vote, when I asked you this question and I'm happy with the answer. In essence, you said it would be so difficult—I'm going to change my wording of it.

It's so difficult to do a matrix for companies to do a matrix to price out the yield curve.

MR. RYAN: Right.

MEMBER GARDENHIRE: That the information really wasn't readily available. Do you agree with that? Do you know how hard it would be to do that?

MR. RYAN: Impossible. First of all, coupon bonds don't go past the 15-year duration, right? So what do you do past 15 years?

MR. MCSHEA: No, you're not following me.

MR. RYAN: Re-state the question please.

MEMBER STEIN: He was asking, can you build a yield curve in your kitchen.

MR. RYAN: Yes, I'm going to get to that stuff. First, you can't do it because there are no bonds past 15 years, right?

MR. MCSHEA: Okay.

MR. RYAN: Okay. Number two is, —

MEMBER STEIN: You're talking about doing that with corporates, right, rather than with —

MR. MCSHEA: Yes, I'm talking about doing it with Treasuries. Can you do it with Treasuries?

MR. RYAN: Absolutely. Treasuries have real zeroes, basically every month of every quarter, going out for 28 years. We had a sad day in the bond business when the Treasury, on Halloween 2001, canceled the 30-year Treasury.

I don't think they realized what they did. It's hard to match liabilities past 28 years now. State lotteries are a great example of what to do. They match assets and liabilities and go to bed, right?

And they're struggling to find Treasuries past 28 years right now. So, if we have it, why create something when we already have it?

We have zeroes every month, every quarter, going out 28 years.

MEMBER GARDENHIRE: One of the questions we asked other people was depth and risk of the corporate bond market, and we basically got an answer that it wasn't very deep at all.

MR. RYAN: Right.

MEMBER STEIN: It is bad breadth.

MEMBER GARDENHIRE: What?

MEMBER STEIN: It is bad breadth.

MEMBER GARDENHIRE: How deep is the corporate Treasury market? I mean, is it deep enough for everybody to step in and do this?

MR. RYAN: How deep is the Treasury market?

MEMBER GARDENHIRE: I mean, compared to the corporates?

MR. RYAN: Oh, it's the biggest market—the largest corporate bonds, until General Motors offered the $13 billion suite of issues—now; most corporate bonds are below $400 million in size. A $1 billion Treasury issue is considered an odd lot.

MEMBER GARDENHIRE: What?

MR. RYAN: A $1 billion Treasury issue is considered an odd lot. We issue $20-25 billion every auction—the size of some countries. So, there's no question that the greatest liquidity in the world is with the Treasury market; the greatest size.

And, God bless America's deficit, we're now going to increase that.

CHAIRPERSON MUIR: I have a follow-up question with a question about the dependents.

MR. RYAN: Yes.

CHAIRPERSON MUIR: And, we've gotten specific information from Lehman Brothers, on the Lehman Brother's long credit securities indices. And I just want to be sure I understand them, the first page of the appendix here, you're talking about the Moody's Aa corporate, which is one that people typically talk about when they talk about what Congress' proposing as the long-term high-grade corporate bond rate.

And then, point number four here, you say there are only 44 bonds that are Aa, with maturities longer than 20 years. And only 16 issues qualify under some other criteria.

Now, again, the lack of breadth, or bad breadth, or something going on there. Can you explain the 16 issues, and can you also talk a little about, if you have it available, the market value of those 44 bonds?

MR. RYAN: This index belongs in a museum, not financial statements. It's old, and that's a problem with it. It only has 20—excuse me, 16 bonds, nine are utilities and seven are industrials.

They all tend to be small issues. Almost half of them have callable features, another distortion. They're only long bonds, no yield curve here. It doesn't include finance, and I think you heard Steve Berkley talk that finance now is the major part of the corporate bond market today.

No finance paper in this index with no zero-coupon bonds, no yield curve, no finance. It's supposed to represent a current yield, but since half of the bonds are callable, it violates its own rules.

It's a mess. It even has a weighting problem, they do equal weighting in a very funny way. They equal weight the utilities, they equal weight the industrials, nine and seven bonds, and then equal weight the two answers.

That's a strange equal weighting. The calculations, I think, are an average yield for the month, not a month-end close, so you couldn't price anything at the market on that day; it's an average for the month.

As you've seen just this month, you know, yields have gone crazy this month. So, I don't think people realize the problem with money. If you're off by 100 basis points in your discount rate, you multiply that times the duration of your liabilities and you get the money.

Most pension funds have durations of 10 to 15 years, so a 1%, a 100 basis point error in price, means 10-15% error in dollars. That's big bucks.

CHAIRPERSON MUIR: So, if you're telling me that the—you're telling me this, and we assume that the 30-year Treasuries are an endangered species that may disappear on us, you're saying that the Moody's Aa corporate bond is what, a dinosaur? The long bond?

MR. RYAN: Yes, that's right. It was in the trashcan, and then corporations were needy, trying to find some yield that would qualify. And they looked in the trashcan and found it.

So, it's not Moody's fault, it's the people who use it.

CHAIRPERSON MUIR: Okay, Norman?

MEMBER STEIN: You would favor, when talking about transition period, you would favor some type of amortization, rather than—

MR. RYAN: I don't like that word, but go ahead.

MEMBER STEIN: Okay, well,—

MR. RYAN: A transition period.

MEMBER STEIN: You would—to make a transition period work, you wouldn't—the Treasury, and most of the witnesses we've heard from, have focused on the corporate bond rate yield—to the extent that we need a period of relatively eased funding, to get from here to there, you would prefer some other mechanism, right, than going to the long interest rate?

MR. RYAN: Yes, I mentioned contributions that—the game is one of money; the game is one of cost.

MEMBER STEIN: Well, the things that I've heard, which I was somewhat sympathetic to, would be to temporarily to reduce the target from 90% to some lower percentage, before deficit funding contributions trigger for amortizing or repress the first four or five years, the first year deficit reduction contribution —

MR. RYAN: To let me understand your words, don't change the price, don't change the discount rate. Change something else.

MEMBER STEIN: Yes.

MR. RYAN: And that something else is the minimum contribution that—

MEMBER STEIN: Either the minimum contribution or the trigger point for making that minimum contribution.

MR. RYAN: Right. But let's make sure we understand clearly the asset/liability and balances. And we should price assets at the market too, rather than smoothing—

MEMBER STEIN: Yes, I know.

MR. RYAN: Yes, we want to know the truth, unlike the Jack Nicholson movie. We want to know the truth, so we can understand our problems and fix them. We want to know the truth, just like a doctor. I want accurate blood work and X-rays, so I can understand how to prescribe medication and cure for this patient.

But it's going to take time to heal, and we'll give you time through other ways, like the minimum contribution.

MEMBER GARDENHIRE: You mentioned knowing the truth. Several people have put forth the idea of transparency; disclose which companies are underfunded. How do you see that helping, hurting or being neutral, the capital markets?

MR. RYAN: Well, after Enron, you would think that Mr. Clean would be the symbol for America today. If you would come clean, and let us know clearly accurate financial statements, you would be blessed, you would be honored in America, rather than can we trust you.

Because we keep reading about this constantly, of financial integrity on financial statements. And, just recently, God bless, it's Freddie Mac. So, America will embrace integrity, financial integrity.

MEMBER GARDENHIRE: It's Freddie Mac, and most new agencies that have those problems, are they AA rated?

MR. RYAN: AAA, government implied, moral obligation.

MEMBER STEIN: That's one reason they had editorials against them, saying what's good for the goose is good for the gander. What they're really saying, I think, is what isn't good shouldn't be good for the gander.

MR. RYAN: I really think America is just fed up and wants to know what's going on, because it affects the stockholders of America. And, it could affect every citizen as they have to pay for it, either in the form of taxes—

MEMBER STEIN: Well, we already have that—

MR. RYAN: Well, there may be more taxes. In the case of PBGC, maybe higher premiums on your payroll. Yes, sir?

MEMBER SZCZUR: So it would be a good idea for the Treasury to start issuing again, 30-year bonds, 40-year bonds, and 50-year bonds?

MR. RYAN: Amen, write your Congressman. It should be a shelf-registration that says we will give you what you want, because you know, we're going to be financing debt for a long time. So, if you need a 37-year zero, you've got it.

MEMBER STEIN: There probably isn't a whole lot of difference in a 30-year and a 37-year. That probably wouldn't—

MR. RYAN: The yield difference might be slight. It's the duration. Remember my little formula?

MEMBER STEIN: If you're actually needing some bonds in your portfolio, you're—

MR. RYAN: Sure.

MEMBER STEIN: —you're just trying to use it as a benchmark; we've got best guesses, probably, for most 30-year Treasuries.

MR. RYAN: And you would think at the lowest rates in 50 years, and a rising deficit, government would say, I'm willing to finance as much as you want here, let's go. But it should be a shelf-registration that would give you what you need, which is really what they did with non-marketables. Yes, sir?

MEMBER SZCZUR: I forgot my question. Oh, I got it. The—some other folks had described that the duration of the liabilities of typical plan is 10 to 15, is that right?

MR. RYAN: That's a fair approximation.

MEMBER SZCZUR: So this kind of gets to the question, that how much the yield curve analysis matters. If the duration, generally of the liabilities, is 10 to 15, and most plans fall in there, and you follow the yield curve, then you're only talking about plans measured in liabilities, the difference being 10 to 15 as a 5% difference versus 2%—

MR. RYAN: Nope.

MEMBER SZCZUR: It's the outliers that would be most impacted by the —

MR. RYAN: Interest rates go up or down 100 basis points, okay, 1%.

MEMBER SZCZUR: Okay.

MR. RYAN: If I have a 10-year duration that means liabilities would change 10%?

MEMBER SZCZUR: Right.

MR. RYAN: If I have 15-year duration, liabilities would change 15%?

MEMBER SZCZUR: Right.

MR. RYAN: See the multiplier effect? Even though interest rates moved 1%, my liabilities moved 5% more.

MEMBER SZCZUR: Right, so if you're measuring—doesn't that imply though that if you're using the yield curve and if the worst case is the plan's liabilities have a duration of 10, and the best case that the duration's 15, that to use the yield curve to get an accurate price, the worst case is they're priced correctly at a duration of 10 instead of 15?

MR. RYAN: You're saying within 5%, is that what you're saying?

MEMBER SZCZUR: Yes.

MR. RYAN: But in dollars, that's a big number. But, yes. And the whole point here is that liabilities are like snowflakes. You'll never see two pension liabilities with the same shape.

And that's why you have to do it customized. To say it differently, I have a pension liability that has an average duration of 10 years. Could I go out and buy 100% 10-year zero-coupon bonds that match that liability?

It doesn't work. It depends on the yield curve, it changes its shape on that match. So, the shape of the yield curve is important, and it's different for every client.

Do yield curves go in reverse? So, that's why we're promoting custom liability indices, that until you take the actuarial schedule, and weigh it—liabilities need to be weighted, not by the market, but by your liabilities.

That's very important.

CHAIRPERSON MUIR: Any final questions?

MR. RYAN: They're worn out.

(Laughter.)

CHAIRPERSON MUIR: I think that's right, thank you very much for coming in and speaking with us today.

MR. RYAN: God bless, thank you.

RYAN ALM GLOSSARY OF PENSION TERMS

A

Accrued Monthly Benefit (AMB) – The monthly pension amount earned by an employee through service with a company.

Accumulated Benefit Obligation – The actuarial present value of benefits (whether vested or nonvested) attributed by the pension benefit formula to employee service rendered before a specified date and based on employee service and compensation (if applicable) prior to that date. The accumulated benefit obligation differs from the projected benefit obligation in that it includes no assumption about future compensation levels. For plans with flat-benefit or non-pay-related pension benefit formulas, the accumulated benefit obligation and the projected benefit obligation are the same.

Actual Return on Plan Assets Component (of net periodic pension cost) – The difference between fair value of plan assets at the end of the period and the fair value at the beginning of the period, adjusted for contributions and payments of benefits during the period.

Actuarial Assumptions – Assumptions as to the occurrence of future events affecting pension costs. These assumptions include rate of mortality, withdrawal, disablement, and retirement. Also included are rates of investment earnings, changes in compensation, as well as statistics related to marriage and family composition.

Actuarial Cost Method – A procedure for determining an allocation of pension costs to each fiscal year. Although all proper cost methods will accumulate sufficient assets to provide for members pensions, some accumulate assets more or less rapidly than others by producing higher or lower costs in the earlier years with corresponding decreasing or increasing costs in future years.

Actuarial Funding Method – Any of several techniques that actuaries use to determine the amounts and incidence of employer contributions to provide for the pension benefits.

Actuarial Present Value – The value, as of a specified date, of an amount or series of amounts payable or receivable thereafter, with each amount adjusted to reflect the time value of money (through accrual of interest) and the probability of payments. For example, if $600 invested today will be worth $1000 in 10 years and if there is a 50% probability that a person will live 10 years, then the actuarial present value of $1000 payable to that person if he should survive 10 years is $300.

Actuarial Present Value – The value, as of a specified date, of an amount or series of amounts payable or receivable thereafter, with each amount adjusted to reflect (a) the time value of money (through discounts for interest), and (b) the probability of payment (by means of decrements for events such as death, disability, withdrawal, or retirement) between the specified date and the expected date of payment.

Actuarial Value of Assets – The value of cash, investments, and other property belonging to the pension plan as used by the actuary for the purpose of the actuarial valuation. The value corresponds to the book value, market value, or some modification involving either or both book and market value.

Allocated contract – A contract with an insurance company under which payments to the insurance company are currently used to purchase immediate or deferred annuities for individual participants.

Alpha – The excess return over the stated objective of the assets. Usually this objective is stated as an index (i.e., generic market index). If assets have a liability driven objective, alpha is the excess return over the growth of liabilities in market value dollars. The growth in liabilities is best measured as a custom liability index since no two liabilities are alike.

Amortization – Usually refers to the process of reducing a recognized liability systematically by recognizing revenues, or reducing a recognized asset systematically by recognizing expenses or costs. In pension accounting, amortization is also used to refer to the systematic recognition in net pension cost over several periods of previously unrecognized amounts, including unrecognized prior service cost and unrecognized net gain or loss.

Amortization Payment – That portion of the pension plan contribution designated to pay interest and reduce the outstanding principal balance of unfunded actuarial accrued liability. If the amortization payment is less than the accrued interest on the unfunded actuarial accrued liability, the outstanding principal balance will increase.

Annuitant – The person receiving payment in annuity form.

Annuity – Periodic payments to a person, usually for life.

Annuity Contract – Annuity contracts are also called allocated contracts. A contract in which an insurance company unconditionally undertakes a legal obligation to provide specified pension benefits to specific individuals in return for a fixed consideration or premium. An annuity contract is irrevocable and involves the transfer of significant risk from the employer to the insurance company.

Asset Gain – That portion of the actuarial gain attributable to investment performance above the expected rate of return in the actuarial assumptions.

Asset Loss – That portion of the actuarial gain attributable to investment performance below the expected rate of return in the actuarial assumptions.

Assumptions – Estimates of the occurrence of future events affecting pension costs, such as mortality, withdrawal, disablement and retirement, changes in compensation and national pension benefits, and discount rates to reflect the time value of money.

Attribution – The process of assigning pension benefits or cost to periods of employee service.

B

Beneficiary – A person designated by a pension plan participant to receive all or a portion of the pension benefit upon the participant's death.

Benefit Approach – One of three groups of basic approaches to attributing pension benefits or costs to periods of employee service. Approaches in the group assign a distinct unit of benefit to each year of credited service. The actuarial present value of that unit of benefit is computed separately and determines the cost assigned to that year. The accumulated benefits approach, benefit/compensation approach, and benefit/years-of-service approach are examples of benefit approaches.

Benefits – Payments to which participants may be entitled under a pension plan, including pension benefits, death benefits, and benefits due on termination of employment.

Benefit Offset – A reduction in a person's pension benefit because he or she owes money to the plan, or is also receiving other benefits. Benefit offset rules are set by the provisions of the person's pension plan.

Benefit/Years-of-Service Approach – One of three benefit approaches. Under this approach, an equal portion of the total estimated benefit is attributed to each year of service. The actuarial present value of the benefits is derived after the benefits are attributed to the periods.

Beta Portfolio – The portfolio of assets that match the risk/reward behavior of the stated objective. Usually this objective is stated as an index (i.e., generic market index). If assets have a liability driven objective, the beta portfolio is the portfolio that matches the present value growth of liabilities in market value dollars.

Bogey – The return or benchmark to which an investment manager's performance is compared.

C

Captive Insurance Subsidiary – An insurance company that does business primarily with related entities.

Career-Average-Pay Formula/Career-Average-Pay-Plan – A benefit formula that bases benefits on the employee's compensation over the entire period of service with the employer. A career-average-pay plan is a plan with such a formula.

Certain and Continuous – An annuity guaranteed to be paid for a specified number of years. If the annuitant dies prior to the specified number of years, his/her beneficiary will receive the annuity for the remaining years.

Contribution Shortfall or Contribution Excess – The difference between contributions recommended in the prior valuation and the actual amount received.

Contributory Plan – A pension plan under which employees contribute part of the cost. In some contributory plans, employees wishing to be covered must contribute; in other contributory plans, employee contributions result in increased benefits.

Cost Approach – One of two groups of basic approaches to attributing pension benefits or costs to periods of service. Approaches in this group assign net pension costs to periods as level amounts or constant percentages of compensation.

Cost/Compensation Approach – One of two cost approaches. Net pension costs under this approach are attributed to periods so that they are a constant percentage of compensation for each period.

Credited Service (CS) – The total time spent working that counts toward the pension benefit. Credited service is most often the number of years worked for a company, up to the date of plan termination, or the date of plan freeze, whichever is earlier. It could be less for certain plans and for employees who worked part-time.

Custom Liability Index (CLI) – The CLI is a portfolio of zero coupon bonds whose par values equal the liability payment amounts and whose maturities match the liability payment dates. Such a portfolio can be priced several different ways depending on the discount rate methodology chosen. A market valuation uses a yield curve of Treasury zero coupon bonds (STRIPS); the PPA uses two valuation methods: a three segment yield curve and a spot yield curve. Both methods are based on hypothetical corporate bond zeroes.

D

Date of Plan Termination – The date a pension plan ended.

Date of Trusteeship – The date that the Pension Benefit Guaranty Corporation (PBGC) takes over the management of a pension plan and its assets, and assumes responsibility for making payments to plan participants.

Defined Benefit Pension Plan – A pension plan that defines an amount of pension benefit to be provided, usually as a function of one or more factors such as age, years of service, or compensation. Any pension plan that is not a defined contribution pension plan is, for purposes of this statement, a defined benefit pension plan.

Defined Contribution Pension Plan – A plan that provides pension benefits in return for services rendered, provides an individual account for each participant, and specifies how contributions to the individual's account are to be determined, instead of specifying the amount of benefits the individual is to receive. Under a defined contribution pension plan, the benefits a participant will receive depend solely on the amount contributed to the participant's account, the returns earned on investments of those contributions, and forfeitures of other participants' benefits that may be allocated to such participant's account.

Discount Rate – The interest rate used to adjust for the time value of money.

Distress Termination – A company-initiated termination of a defined benefit pension plan typically occurring when the company is in financial difficulty, and/or the pension plan does not have enough assets to pay all current and future benefits, where as continuing the plan would likely force the company to shut down.

E

Employee Retirement Income Security Act (ERISA) – The federal law that establishes the basic requirements for employee benefit plans. The authority for administering and enforcing ERISA is divided among three federal agencies: the Internal Revenue Service (IRS), the Department of Labor (DOL), and the Pension Benefit Guaranty Corporation (PBGC).

Employer Normal Cost – That portion of the normal cost not attributable to employee contributions. It includes both direct contributions made by the employer and contributions from other non-employee sources such as revenue sharing and revenues related to taxes.

Expected Long-Term Rate of Return on Plan Assets – An assumption as to the rate of return on plan assets reflecting the average rate of earnings expected on the funds invested or to be invested to provide for the benefits included in the projected benefit obligation.

Expected Return on Plan Assets – An amount calculated as a basis for determining the extent of delayed recognition of the effects of changes in the fair value of assets. The expected return on plan assets is determined based on the expected long-term rate of return on plan assets and the market-related value of plan assets.

Explicit Approach to Assumptions – An approach under which each significant assumption used reflects the best estimate of the plan's future experience solely with respect to that assumption.

F

Fair Value – The amount that a pension plan could reasonably expect to receive for an investment in a current sale between a willing buyer and a willing seller, that is, other than in a forced or liquidation sale.

Fiduciary – With regard to a pension plan, a person or organization with control over the plan or its assets.

Final-Pay Formula/Final-Pay Plan – A benefit formula that bases benefits on the employee's compensation over a specified number of years near the end of the employee's service period or on the employee's highest compensation periods. For example, a plan might provide annual pension benefits equal to 1% of the employee's average salary for the last five years (or the highest consecutive five years) for each year of service. A final-pay plan is a plan with such a formula.

Flat-Benefit Formula/Flat-Benefit Plan – A benefit formula that bases benefits on a fixed amount per year of service, such as $20 of monthly retirement income for each year of credited service. A flat-benefit plan is a plan with such a formula.

Flat-Rate Premium – The premium rate that pension plans pay annually to PBGC for each plan participant. The rate is different for multiemployer plans versus single-employer plans.

Fully Funded – A pension plan with sufficient assets to pay all current and future benefits.

Fund – *v.* To pay over to a funding agency (as to fund future pension benefits or to fund pension cost). *–n.* Assets accumulated in the hands of a funding agency for the purpose of meeting pension benefits when they become due.

Funded Ratio – The value of assets divided by the value of liabilities expressed as a percentage. A ratio less than 100% is considered to have a deficit equal to the difference from 100%. Such a calculation can be based on *actuarial valuations or market valuations.* Actuarial valuations use smoothing techniques over two years on assets and hypothetical discount rates on liabilities. Market valuations use real and current asset valuations plus market interest rates as the discount rates for liabilities.

Funding Policy – The program regarding the amounts and timing of contributions by the employer(s), participants, and any other sources (for example, state subsidies or federal grants) to provide specific pension plan benefits.

G

Gain or Loss – A change in the value of either the projected benefit obligation or the plan assets, resulting from an experience different from that assumed, or from a change in an actuarial assumption.

Gain or Loss Component (of net periodic pension cost) – The sum of (a) the difference between the actual return on plan assets and the expected return on plan assets and (b) the amortization of the unrecognized net gain or loss from previous periods. The gain or loss component is the net effect of delayed recognition of gains and losses (the net change in the unrecognized net gain or loss), except that it does not include changes in the projected benefit obligation, which occur during the period and are deferred for later recognition.

I

Implicit Approach to Assumptions – An approach under which two or more assumptions do not individually represent the best estimate of the plan's future experience with respect to those assumptions. Instead, the aggregate effect of their combined use is presumed to be approximately the same as that produced by an explicit approach.

Interest Cost Component (of net periodic pension cost) – The increase in the projected benefit obligation due to passage of time.

Involuntary Termination – A PBGC-initiated termination of an underfunded defined benefit pension plan.

J

Joint-and-Survivor Annuity – An annuity paying one individual for his or her life and then providing for an annuity for the person's surviving spouse, usually in a reduced amount.

L

Lump Sum Payment – When a participant receives a benefit all at once, as opposed to receiving regular installments.

M

Market-Related Value of Plan Assets (MVA) – A balance used to calculate the expected return on plan assets. Market-related value can be either fair market value or a calculated value that recognizes changes in fair value in a systematic and rational manner over not more than five years. Different ways of calculating market-related value may be used for different classes of assets, but the manner of determining market-related value shall be applied consistently from year to year for each asset class.

Market-Related Value of ABO Liabilities (MVABO) – A calculation of the present value (market value) of liabilities using a yield curve of hypothetical AA corporate zero-coupon bonds in conformity with ASC 715 (FAS No. 158) with a base of real corporate bond rates.

Maximum Guaranteed Benefit – Under the law, the largest monthly amount PBGC can pay a participant from its funds.

Measurement Date – The date as of which plan assets and obligations are measured.

Mortality Rate – The proportion of the number of deaths in a specified group to the number living at the beginning of the period in which the deaths occur. Actuaries use mortality tables, which show death rates for each age, in estimating the amount of pension benefits that will become payable.

Multiemployer Plan – A pension plan to which two or more unrelated employers contribute, usually pursuant to one or more collective-bargaining agreements. A characteristic of multiemployer plans is that assets contributed by one participating employer may be used to provide benefits to employees of other participating employers since assets contributed by an employer are not segregated in a separate account or restricted to provide benefits only to employees of that employer. A multiemployer plan is usually administered by a board of trustees composed of management and labor representatives and may also be referred to as a "joint trust" or "union" plan. Generally, many employers participate in a multiemployer plan, and an employer may participate in more than one plan. The employers participating in multiemployer plans usually have a common industry bond, but for some plans the employers are in different industries and the labor union may be their only common bond.

Multiple-Employer Plan – A pension plan maintained by more than one employer but not treated as a multiemployer plan. Multiple-employer plans are not as prevalent as single-employer and multiemployer plans, but some of the ones that do exist are large and involve many employers. Multiple-employer plans are generally not collectively bargained and are intended to allow participating employers, commonly in the same industry, to pool their assets for investment purposes and reduce the costs of plan administration. A multiple-employer plan maintains separate accounts for each employer so that contributions provide benefits only for employees of the contributing employer. Some multiple-employer plans have features that allow participating employers to have different benefit formulas, with the employer's contributions to the plan based on the benefit formula selected by the employer.

N

Net Periodic Pension Cost – The amount recognized in an employer's financial statements as the cost of a pension plan for a period. Components of net periodic pension cost are service cost, interest cost, actual return on plan assets, gain or loss, amortization of unrecognized prior service cost, and amortization of the unrecognized net obligation or asset existing at the date of initial application of this statement. We use the term *net periodic pension cost* instead of *net pension expense* because part of the cost recognized in a period may be capitalized along with other costs as part of an asset such as inventory.

Nonparticipating Annuity Contract – An annuity contract that does not provide for the purchaser to participate in the investment performance or in other experience of the insurance company.

Nonpublic Enterprise – An enterprise other than one (a) whose debt or equity securities are traded in a public market, either on a stock exchange or in the over-the-counter market (including securities quoted only locally or regionally), or (b) whose financial statements are filed with a regulatory agency in preparation for the sale of any class of securities.

Normal Cost – That portion of the actuarial present value of pension plan benefits and expenses allocated to a valuation year by the actuarial cost method. This is analogous to one year's insurance premium.

P

Participant – Any employee or former employee, or any member or former member of a trade or other employee association, or the beneficiaries of those individuals, for whom there are pension plan benefits.

Participant – A person who is or may become eligible to receive a benefit from a pension plan.

Participating Annuity Contract – An annuity contract that provides for the purchaser to participate in the investment performance and possibly other experience (for example, mortality experience) of the insurance company.

Participation Right – A purchaser's right under a participating contract to receive future dividends or retroactive rate credits from the insurance company.

PBGC – The Pension Benefit Guaranty Corporation, a federal government agency that insures private defined benefit pension plans.

Pension Benefit Formula/Plan's Benefit Formula/Benefit Formula – The basis for determining payments for which participants may be entitled under a pension plan. Pension benefit formulas usually refer to the employee's service or compensation, or both.

Pension Benefit Obligation – The actuarial present value of benefits earned or credited to date based on the member's expected final average compensation at retirement. For retired or terminated members, this is equivalent to the actuarial present value of the members accrued benefit.

Pension Benefits – Periodic (usually monthly) payments made pursuant to the terms of the pension plan to a person who has retired from employment, or to that person's beneficiary.

Performance Attribution Report (PAR) – PAR compares the risk/reward behavior of any two portfolios. Ryan ALM uses PAR to compare assets to their stated index objective. For liability driven objectives, PAR compares assets versus liabilities as measured by a custom liability index. PAR calculates eight measurements of relative risk, four measurements of relative reward, and two measurements of risk-adjusted returns.

Plan Administrator – The person, committee, or company designated to manage a pension plan's daily business.

Plan Amendment – A change in the terms of an existing pension plan or the initiation of a new pension plan. A plan amendment may increase benefits, including those attributed to years of service already rendered.

Plan Assets – Assets (typically in the form of stocks, bonds, and other investments) that have been segregated and restricted (usually in a trust) to provide benefits. Plan assets include amounts contributed by the employer (as well as by employees for a contributory plan) and amounts earned from investing the contributions, less benefits paid. Plan assets cannot ordinarily be withdrawn by the employer except in certain circumstances when a plan has assets in excess of obligations and the employer has taken certain steps to satisfy existing obligations. For purposes of this statement, assets not segregated in a trust or otherwise effectively restricted so that they cannot be used by the employer for other purposes are not plan assets even though it may be intended that such assets be used to provide pensions.

Amounts accrued by the employer as net periodic pension cost but not yet paid to the plan are not plan assets, provided they are transferable. If a plan has liabilities other than for benefits, those non-benefit obligations may be considered as reductions of plan assets for purposes of this statement.

Plan Curtailment – An event that significantly reduces the expected years of future service of present employees or eliminates for a significant number of employees the accrual of defined benefits for some or all of their future services.

Plan Sponsor (for a multiemployer plan) – The board of trustees that oversees a multiemployer pension plan.

Plan Sponsor (for a single-employer plan) – An employer that establishes or maintains a pension plan for its employees.

Plan Suspension – An event in which the pension plan is frozen and no further benefits accrue. Future service may continue to be the basis for vesting of non-vested benefits existing at the date of suspension. The plan may still hold assets, pay benefits already accrued, and receive additional employer contributions for any unfunded benefits. Employees may or may not continue working for the employer.

Plan Termination – An event in which the pension plan ceases to exist and all benefits are settled by purchase of annuities or other means. The plan may or may not be replaced by another plan. A plan termination with a replacement plan may or may not be in substance a plan termination for accounting purposes.

Prepaid Pension Cost – Cumulative employer contributions in excess of accrued net pension cost.

Prior Service Cost – The cost of retroactive benefits granted in a plan amendment.

Projected Benefit Obligation – The actuarial present value as of a date of all benefits attributed by the pension benefit formula to employee service rendered prior to that date. The projected benefit obligation is measured using assumptions as to future compensation levels (pay-related, final-pay, final-average-pay, or career-average-pay plans).

Q

Qualified Domestic Relations Order (QDRO) – A court order, usually in a divorce case, that meets legal requirements for awarding some or all of a participant's pension benefits to the participant's spouse, former spouse, child, or other dependent.

R

Retroactive Benefits – Benefits granted in a plan amendment (or initiation) that are attributed by the pension benefit formula to employee services rendered in periods prior to the amendment. The cost of the retroactive benefits is referred to as prior service cost.

ROA – Return on Asset Assumption.

Ryan Asset Allocation Model (RAAM) – Based on data from a custom liability index, the RAAM calculates the economic funded ratio in market value dollars. Based on this funded ratio, the ROA and the time horizon used (average duration of liabilities or the PPA requirement), the RAAM calculates the allocation to alpha and beta assets.

S

Service – Employment taken into consideration under a pension plan. Years of employment before the inception of a pension plan constitute an employee's *past service*; years thereafter are classified in relation to the particular actuarial valuation being made or discussed. Years of employment (including past service) prior to the date of a particular valuation constitute *prior service*; years of employment following the date of the valuation constitute *future service*; a year of employment adjacent to the date of valuation, or in which such date falls, constitutes *current service*.

Service Cost Component (of net periodic pension cost) – The actuarial present value of benefits attributed by the pension benefit formula to services rendered by employees during that period. The service cost component is a portion of the projected benefit obligation and is unaffected by the funded status of the plan.

Settlement – An irrevocable action that relieves the employer (or the pension plan) of primary responsibility for a pension benefit obligation and eliminates significant risks related to the obligation and the assets used to effect the settlement. Examples of transactions that constitute a settlement include: making lump-sum cash payments to plan participants in exchange for their rights to receive specified pension benefits, and purchasing nonparticipating annuity contracts to cover vested benefits.

Single-Employer Plan – A pension plan sponsored by a single employer or a group of companies under common control. Also, a pension plan sponsored by unrelated companies that is not collectively bargained.

Single Life Annuity – Periodic payments for the life of the participant with no benefits payable after the participant's death.

Sponsor/Pension Plan Sponsor – In the case of a pension plan established or maintained by a single employer, the employer is referred to as the sponsor or pension plan sponsor. In the case of a plan established or maintained jointly by one or more employers or employee organizations, the association, committee, joint board of trustees, or other group of representatives of the parties who have established or who maintain the pension plan is referred to as the sponsor or pension plan sponsor.

Standard Termination – Termination of a plan that has enough assets to pay for all benefits.

Surviving Spouse – The living spouse of a deceased participant. A Qualified Domestic Relations Order (QDRO) may treat a participant's former spouse as a surviving spouse.

T

Termination (for single-employer plans) – When a pension plan ends.

Trustee – A person or organization with a duty to receive, manage, and disburse the assets of a pension plan.

Turnover – Termination of employment for a reason other than death or retirement.

U

Unallocated Contract – A contract with an insurance company under which payments to the insurance company are accumulated in an unallocated fund (not allocated to specific plan participants) to be used either directly or through the purchase of annuities, to meet benefit payments when employees retire. Funds held by the insurance company under an unallocated contract may be withdrawn and otherwise invested.

Underfunded Plan – A pension plan without enough assets to pay all benefits.

Unfunded Accrued Pension Cost – Cumulative net pension cost accrued in excess of the employer's contributions.

Unfunded Accumulated Benefit Obligation – The excess of the accumulated benefit obligation over plan assets.

Unfunded Actuarial Accrued Liability – The excess of the actuarial accrued liability over the actuarial value of assets.

Unfunded Projected Benefit Obligation – The excess of the projected benefit obligation over plan assets.

Unrecognized Net Gain or Loss – The cumulative net gain or loss that has not been recognized as a part of net periodic pension cost.

Unrecognized Prior Service Cost – That portion of prior service cost that has not been recognized as a part of net periodic pension cost.

V

Variable-Rate Premium (single-employer plans) – Additional premium amount, based on the amount of the plan's unfunded benefit liabilities, that an underfunded plan or its sponsor must pay to PBGC.

Vested Benefits – Benefits for which the employee's right to receive a present or future pension benefit is no longer contingent on remaining in the service of the employer. Other conditions, such as inadequacy of the pension fund, may prevent the employee from receiving the vested benefit. Under *graded vesting*, the initial *vested right* may be to receive in the future a stated percentage of a pension based on the number of years of accumulated credited service; thereafter, the percentage may increase with the number of years of service (or of age) until the right to receive the entire benefit has vested.

Vested Rights – A promise made to employees by an employer that is legally enforced. Such vested rights are assets that cannot be taken away by any third party even though one may not yet possess the asset. The portion of assets vested cannot be reclaimed by the employer, nor can it be used to satisfy the employer's debts.

INDEX

M

N

O

P

R

S

T

U

V

W

Y

Z

About the Author

A recipient of the financial industry's prestigious William F. Sharpe Index Lifetime Achievement Award and many other industry accolades, Ron Ryan is a respected financial asset/liability expert. He is the CEO and founder of Ryan ALM, Inc., a bond asset/liability advisory and bond index firm that provides major financial indexes and strategies for pensions and ETFs. With a background that includes creator of three fixed income firms, director of research at Lehman Brothers, head of Texas' largest fixed income trust department, and security analyst at Louisiana's largest institutional investment entity, he is eminently qualified to sound the alarm on the current state of the U.S. pension crisis. Over the span of his 45+ year career, Ryan and his associates have designed and implemented numerous bond indexes and investment strategies.

Send your questions and comments to contact@RyanALM.com

To subscribe to Ron Ryan's quarterly pension newsletter, ***The Ryan Letter***, plus receive access to timely Pension White Papers, subscribe to the Ryan ALM email list at **www.RyanALM.com**